Double Visi

A comedy

Eric Chappell

Samuel French — London
New York - Toronto - Hollywood

DOUBLE VISION

First produced as a rehearsed reading by *productionline* at the Unity Theatre, Liverpool, on 6th February 2001 with the following cast:

Spinks	Frank Miles
Kingsley	Sean Halligan
Dawn Pringle	Joanne Sherryden
Donna Miller	Joanne Sherryden

Directed by Paul Goetzee
Lighting by Paul Skinner
Stage management by Sam Barron

Subsequently produced at the Robin Hood Theatre, Averham, on 31st May 2001 with the following cast:

Spinks	David Hawley
Kingsley	Kerry Dracott
Dawn Pringle	Ellie Doherty
Donna Miller	Ellie Doherty

Directed by Val Wilson
Designed by Keith Wilson
Lighting by Michael Dobbs

CHARACTERS

Spinks, untidy, ex-boxer; 50s
Kingsley, rakish, haggard, heavy drinker, about 40
Dawn Pringle, pale and respectable; about 40*
Donna Miller, Dawn's twin sister, flirtatious, manipulative. Played by the actress who plays Dawn*

* See p.vi for an Author's Note concerning these characters

The action of the play takes place in Spinks's council flat in outer London

SYNOPSIS OF SCENES

ACT I

ACT II

AUTHOR'S NOTE

Dawn and Donna

In programmes for **DOUBLE VISION** Dawn and Donna should be billed separately (as pp. iii and v) with the actress's name repeated; this alerts the audience to the fact that one actress is to play both sisters but does not give away their secret.

Eric Chappell

Also by Eric Chappell
published by Samuel French Ltd

Fiddler's Three
Haunted
Haywire
Heatstroke
It Can Damage Your Health
Natural Causes
Something's Burning
Theft
Up and Coming

ACT I
SCENE 1

The main room of a council flat in a high-rise block in outer London. Late afternoon. Autumn

A door UR leads off to the hall, bathroom and bedrooms. A door DR leads into the kitchen. Further DR is a notional balcony door opening DS with, further DS, an open balustrade indicating a narrow balcony. The room is large and untidy, with a fireplace (in which is an electric fire), an old dining-table and chairs, a battered settee, a coffee table, a bin and a sideboard which is covered in bric-a-brac, old photographs and boxing trophies; it also has a teapot on it. Most of the surfaces of the room are covered with pots and plates and clothes; all the debris of an untidy, bachelor existence. The telephone, however, is a state-of-the-art affair, brand new, with an answering machine. A pair of boxing gloves hangs from the wall; also a mirror

When the CURTAIN rises, the electric fire glows in the grate. A discarded shirt covers the telephone

Spinks sits reading a newspaper with the aid of a magnifying glass, and eating beans from a tin. Spinks is in his fifties and is as untidy as the room. His face has the battered look of a boxer who has been in too many fights

There is the sound of the front door opening, off

Spinks glances up with a cynical smile. He puts down the magnifying glass and continues to study the paper without it

Kingsley enters from the hall. He is about forty. He has the rakish appearance and haggard looks of a man who drinks too much. He is huddled inside his topcoat as if he feels the cold. He sits, thrusting his hands deep inside his pockets

Spinks What do you want?
Kingsley You shouldn't say that.
Spinks What?
Kingsley "What do you want?" like that. It's not very friendly. I might stop calling.
Spinks Good.
Kingsley "What do you want?" implies the person calling is after something.

Spinks Well, aren't you?
Kingsley No. I've brought you something. (*He produces a bottle of Scotch from a deep pocket and reaches around for glasses*)
Spinks What's this for?
Kingsley I thought we might be celebrating …
Spinks (*briefly*) Did you? (*He returns to the paper*)

Kingsley finds glasses, pours the drinks and hands one to Spinks. He studies Spinks

Kingsley You should be wearing your glasses, Spinks.
Spinks I don't need them. A bit of double vision, that's all.
Kingsley That's not what Mr Patel says. He says, you should have a white stick.
Spinks A white stick! Do me a favour. That's an invitation to a mugging around here. A white stick! They'd beat you to death with it. I don't need a white stick — I need a swordstick.

Kingsley drinks deep and shakes his head

Kingsley You know, you should really try and get over this distrust of people.
Spinks Why?
Kingsley You're alone in the world — you need friends.
Spinks I've never needed them before. I can count my friends on one hand and still have five fingers left.
Kingsley (*after a pause*) One of those is a thumb.
Spinks A thumb counts as a finger.
Kingsley Are you sure?
Spinks Consult your dictionary. You don't know everything.
Kingsley I know you need friends. Still, all that's going to change, isn't it? (*He studies Spinks*) From what I've heard …
Spinks Is that why you're here?
Kingsley No. I'm your key holder. I'm concerned. We should be concerned about our elderly neighbours. Suppose you collapsed? Have you got a red card to put in the window?
Spinks (*staring*) I'm ten floors up! Who's going to see it? The bloody pigeons?

They drink in silence. Kingsley continues to watch Spinks curiously. He takes two cigars from his pocket

Kingsley Would you like one of these?

Spinks (*taking a cigar with a cynical smile*) First the whisky — now the cigars. Whatever next?

Kingsley Well, from what I've heard — this is a special occasion ...

Spinks Is it?

Spinks returns to his paper. Kingsley continues to study him

Kingsley You can't read that, can you?

Spinks Yes, I can. It's about this woman who lost her head in Harrods.

Kingsley (*shrugging*) They'd steal anything these days. (*He looks around for an ashtray and sees the telephone under the shirt*) Oh, is that the new phone?

Spinks Blimey! It's been in a fortnight. Have you only just noticed it?

Kingsley You had your shirt on it. (*He examines the phone*) Very nice. A nice piece of equipment there, Spinks.

Spinks (*proudly*) Phone and answering machine. Hi-tech. Digital. Recall button. Memo. Volume control. State of the art. He's going mad across the landing — makes his look very basic.

Kingsley What's the tone like?

Spinks I don't know — it hasn't rung yet.

Kingsley (*staring*) It's been in a fortnight and it hasn't rung! I'll go to a call box.

Spinks Don't bother.

Kingsley (*after a pause*) Well, that's another thing that's going to change ...

Spinks Is it?

Kingsley (*feeling in his pocket*) I don't seem to have a light, Spinks ...

Spinks Haven't you?

Spinks takes out a five pound note and folds it neatly. He then lights it from the electric fire. Kingsley watches him in silence. Spinks lights their cigars. Kingsley draws thoughtfully on his cigar

Kingsley Spinks ...

Spinks Yeah?

Kingsley You've just lit our cigars with a five pound note. Either your eyesight is getting worse, or what I've heard is true.

Spinks There's nothing wrong with my eyesight. I just wanted to know what it felt like.

Kingsley You know what it feels like. You did it in the *Horse and Jockey*.

Spinks Anyone can do it once. I wanted to know what it felt like to do it twice.

Kingsley Twice as bloody loony, I should think. (*Pause*) It must be a considerable sum ...

Spinks remains silent

How much was it?

Spinks That's my affair. It pays to be discreet in these matters.

Kingsley Discreet! You've just lit your cigar with a fiver! You did the same in the *Jockey*. I don't call that discreet. I call that getting carried away.

Spinks Well, I'm entitled to a little display — I'm only human. I hope it wasn't too ostentatious, Kingsley.

Kingsley All right. Was it five figures?

Spinks examines his cigar

Six?

Spinks blows out a leisurely cloud of smoke

Not seven! Don't tell me it's seven, Spinks.

Spinks It was a rollover week, wasn't it? Millions in the kitty …

Kingsley (*drinking deeper*) You don't mean I'm looking at a millionaire?

Spinks It's a vulgar term, Kingsley, but I can't put it any other way.

Kingsley whistles

Kingsley A million! (*He looks around the squalid flat*) It's going to change your life, Spinks.

Spinks Of course it's going to change my bleeding life. Have you seen a life that needs changing more than mine does?

Kingsley You're right. That's what everyone's saying. You deserve it, Spinks. A million. And I bought the ticket. That makes me feel part of it.

Spinks (*staring*) Part of it?

Kingsley Almost as if I'd won.

Spinks Well, I'd get over that feeling if I were you — it could lead to disappointment.

Kingsley Wait a minute. You're not suggesting ——

Spinks I'm not suggesting anything.

Kingsley Just remember I was your friend before this happened. I was your friend when you had nothing. It's not me you have to worry about. (*He takes another deep drink*)

Spinks observes the falling level in the bottle

Let me give you a word of warning. Be on your guard.

Spinks I am on my guard.

Kingsley Money changes people. And I'm not talking about the people who win it. I mean those friends who become so jealous they can barely speak to you. (*Darkly*) And the other friends — begging all the time …

Spinks (*after a pause*) Which one are you?

Kingsley Neither. I'm not going to let this make any difference to our relationship.

Spinks Well, that's a relief.

Kingsley All I'm saying is, be on your guard. (*He pours another drink, clinking the neck of the bottle on the glass*) Avoid new acquaintances — any premature attachments. Once this gets round …

Spinks It won't. I insisted on complete confidentiality.

Kingsley (*incredulously*) What's the point in insisting on complete confidentiality when you're lighting your cigars with fivers. It's all round the building. Everyone's talking about it.

Spinks (*pleased*) Are they?

Kingsley I just hope you're going to be sensible. Invest it wisely. Government stocks — gilt edged — quality shares.

Spinks I don't know about shares. What about the last crash?

Kingsley You mean Black Monday?

Spinks Monday? The whole week was a bloody disaster from what I heard. Bloke across the landing went demented. Until then he was always coming across here to show me his unit trusts — saying how well he was doing, how he was making money even when he was in bed — which was most of the time. But after Black Monday he went strangely quiet. He declined faster than the shares. Every night when he watched the stock exchange report, I could hear him shrieking in horror.

Kingsley But he didn't lose any money, Spinks.

Spinks Didn't he?

Kingsley No. He'd have only lost money if he'd sold them.

Spinks Sold them! He couldn't give them away,

Kingsley But they went up again.

Spinks And what goes up — must come down.

Kingsley Then what are you going to do with it?

Spinks Something you may consider unorthodox.

Kingsley What's that?

Spinks Spend it.

Kingsley Not tonight. (*He drains his glass*)

Spinks What do you mean?

Kingsley I mean, your money's no good tonight, Spinks. I'm taking you out. We're going to celebrate — and it's on me. And in the future, when you're surrounded by your fine, new friends — which you will be — remember tonight, the last time you enjoyed genuine friendship.

Spinks (*smiling*) Actually, there are several people who want to take me out tonight, Kingsley.

Kingsley (*fiercely*) I'm taking you out tonight.

The phone rings. Spinks stares at Kingsley

Spinks What's that?
Kingsley It's the phone.
Spinks So that's what it sounds like.
Kingsley See what I mean? It's started.

Spinks answers the phone. Kingsley grimaces and shakes his head during this conversation

Spinks (*into the phone*) Hallo? .. Yeah? … That's me. … Dawn who? Pringle? … No, I know we haven't. … From where? … Oh, yeah. … What now? I don't see why not. I'm not going anywhere. Come on up. … Ten-o-three. Opposite the lift. … Right. (*He hangs up*)
Kingsley Well, she hasn't wasted any time. That was a big mistake, asking her up.
Spinks She sounded agitated.
Kingsley Agitated! You'll be agitated when she's finished with you. It's got around, Spinks. She's after your money.
Spinks How do you know?
Kingsley Because all the time I've known you, Spinks — I've never known a woman come to this flat.
Spinks That's not my fault. I'm ten floors up. By the time they get here they're suffering from lack of oxygen and weightlessness.
Kingsley Well, she seems prepared to make the effort — and you don't even know her.
Spinks She comes from Bromley way. Isn't that where you came from, Kingsley?
Kingsley (*frowning*) I've told you before — Bromley's a closed book as far as I'm concerned.
Spinks I thought you might know her.
Kingsley I don't have to know her. There's a certain woman who preys on people like you, Spinks. I can just see her. Openly seductive — sexually challenging.
Spinks (*intrigued*) Sexually challenging?
Kingsley She'll sway in here, pelvis pressed forward, perfumed and red-lipped — everything moving at once.
Spinks Get away. (*He searches the sideboard*)
Kingsley You won't know whether it's Easter or Christmas. (*Curiously*) What are you looking for?

Spinks produces a cologne bottle

Spinks I knew I'd got it somewhere.
Kingsley What is it?

Spinks (*opening the bottle*) Patchouli oil.

Kingsley It stinks.

Spinks Bound to be a bit volatile. It's been in the bottle for fifteen years. (*He pats the oil on his cheeks*) Now, if you don't mind, Kingsley … (*He attempts to tidy the room during the following*)

Kingsley I'm not leaving you alone with her.

Spinks Why not?

Kingsley Because you could be in moral danger. I owe it to your mother to stay.

Spinks Don't bring her into it.

Kingsley You could get yourself into trouble. That patchouli oil isn't the only thing that's been bottled up for fifteen years.

Spinks (*sighing*) Kingsley, just because I made you my key holder, it doesn't mean you have to use it all the time. You spend more time in this flat than I do. I have to keep checking to see whose name's in the rent book. Don't tell me they've cut your heating off again?

Kingsley No, but I can't get any peace down there, Spinks. Not since he moved in next door with the drum kit.

Spinks Well, talk to him about it.

Kingsley I have done. He says he's going through an emotional crisis. I said, that's no reason for both of us to go through it. But he won't listen. He won't even use the brushes — it's all heavy drum rolls and cymbals.

Spinks Well, that's not my problem.

The doorbell rings

Kingsley I'll get it. (*He moves to the hall door*) After all, you'll have to get used to people opening doors for you …

Kingsley exits into the hall

Spinks smooths his hair down nervously. He moves around the room, loosening up, boxer-style. He throws a few shadow punches

Kingsley returns with Dawn Pringle. He is smiling because Dawn is the complete opposite of the woman he described. She is pale and respectable. Her hair is swept back. She is about forty. She is carrying a newspaper. She appears nervous. She moves to the window and looks out

Spinks and Kingsley exchange glances

Spinks Can I help you, Miss —— ?

Dawn Dawn. Dawn Pringle.

Spinks Yeah. You told me that on the phone.

Dawn First of all, I'd like to congratulate you on your good fortune, Mr Spinks.

Spinks How did you know about it?

Dawn It was in the evening paper.

Spinks What!

Kingsley Let me see. (*He takes the paper and studies it*) There's even a picture! It's not bad. You look a bit cross-eyed, that's all. (*Reading*) "Ex-boxer's lottery win rumoured at over a million. 'I'm off the ropes at last,' beamed three times ABA finalist, Arthur Spinks."

Dawn (*impressed*) Three times! Isn't that splendid?

Kingsley (*coldly*) He never won it.

Spinks Where did they get it from? That's what I want to know.

Kingsley Where do you think? You've been talking, haven't you? (*He continues reading*) "'I'm off the ropes at last,' beamed three times ABA finalist, Arthur Spinks. 'Now it's going to be spend, spend, spend.'"

Spinks I never said that.

Kingsley No, you were too busy insisting on complete confidentiality. (*He reads on*) "Spinks, who fought Kid Fletcher — the future world champion — in three of the most punishing encounters ever seen in the amateur ring, and who later had a long, if undistinguished, professional career" ——

Spinks Undistinguished!

Kingsley — "which left him with failing eyesight."

Spinks (*angrily*) There's nothing wrong with my eyesight!

Dawn I think it's wonderful. So deserving.

Spinks glares at Dawn

When I read about it, I was so pleased for you. Alone, and out of work, and with your failing … (*she becomes aware of Spinks' look*) … thing. I thought, splendid.

Spinks (*unimpressed*) Did you?

Dawn If anyone deserved it, it's you, Mr Spinks. After all you've been through.

Spinks I've never complained.

Dawn No, of course not — you're not the sort.

Spinks In each life a little rain must fall, I know that.

Kingsley Or God wouldn't have given us umbrellas.

Spinks (*frowning*) I'm not keeping you, am I, Kingsley?

Kingsley No.

Dawn You're obviously a person who makes the best of things. Like my aunt. Partially sighted. Permanent limp. Widowed in the war. Second husband an alcoholic. Divorced. Nervous breakdown. Daughter on drugs. Still smiling.

Spinks and Kingsley stare at Dawn in awed silence

Spinks Still smiling?

Kingsley That's not a little rain — that's a downpour.

Spinks (*frowning*) Are you sure you don't have to be somewhere, Kingsley?

Kingsley No. (*He smiles at Dawn*) We're forgetting our manners, Spinks. Would you like a drink, Dawn?

Dawn (*after a hesitation*) Well, tea would be nice …

Kingsley (*staring*) Tea?

Spinks (*grinning*) Do you remember how to make it?

Kingsley Of course. (*He moves to the teapot*)

Spinks (*quickly*) No — not that one. (*He smiles at Dawn*) The dainty one, with the rosebuds, in the kitchen.

Kingsley exits into the kitchen

Dawn I could certainly do with a cup. (*She moves back to the window*)

Spinks watches Dawn curiously

Spinks Are you all right, miss? You seem agitated.

Dawn (*with a nervous laugh*) Agitated! I was born agitated. Agitated is my middle name, Mr Spinks. I've always been agitated.

Spinks (*after a pause*) Well, we seem to have established you're agitated. Question is, why?

Dawn returns from the window and examines the boxing gloves

Dawn So you were a professional boxer, Mr Spinks?

Spinks Only part time. I worked on the railway. The last of the fighting firemen. I was on the footplate before diesel. I've shovelled coal all the way from London to Edinburgh. I should have been a driver but … (*He shrugs*)

Dawn Was it because of your ——

Spinks glares at Dawn. She becomes aware of this

—— disability?

Spinks You need good eyesight on the foot-plate. If you can't see the signals it's frigging chaos. And I couldn't carry on firing. Failure to observe a low tunnel and I could have found my head on the shovel.

Dawn Is that what fighting did to you?

Spinks I wasn't bad. But I kept meeting Fletcher — and he could punch. When he connected the lights went out all over Europe.

Dawn Why didn't you stop?

Spinks Dad always said we could take him. He always said we, but he didn't
have to get in the ring with him. I never did take him. He went on to become
world champion.

Dawn What about your mother? Didn't she worry about you getting hurt —
even disfigured?

Spinks Not really. Well, it wasn't as if I was a beautiful child or anything.
(*He motions to a photograph on the sideboard*) That's my mother, with her
sisters. She's the one who's scowling.

Dawn What about girlfriends? Surely they were concerned. There must have
been girlfriends.

Spinks (*uneasily*) Not in those days. Not with the shift work and the training.
Besides, Dad said they'd soften me up. I don't know why he worried, I
thought Fletcher was doing a good enough job on his own account. Mind
you, the old lady agreed with him. She said women were only after my
money.

Dawn You didn't believe that, surely?

Spinks Why not? The old lady certainly was. If anyone was going to get it,
she was first in line. I didn't know what she did with it. I never saw any of
it. My mother taught me to expect nothing from life — and then made
damned sure I wasn't disappointed.

Dawn And so you never married?

Spinks (*awkwardly*) No.

Dawn And there's no permanent relationship …

Spinks Well, I don't get out much these days. Have you seen the traffic out
there? They drive like maniacs.

Dawn Some drivers have no consideration.

Spinks Right. (*He gives a sly grin*) Although I get my own back. I press the
pedestrian button and don't cross. That gets up their noses.

Dawn They have no thought of others. They don't think there may be people
… Perhaps if you had a dog?

Spinks A dog?

Dawn A blind dog. (*She giggles nervously*) Well, not a blind dog. Not much
point in having a blind dog. You'd both be walking into things. No, I meant
a seeing dog … I, er … (*Her voice tails away in embarrassment*)

Spinks I've only known you a short time, Miss, but I must say you're one
of the most tactless people I've ever met.

Dawn (*sighing*) Oh dear. Dawn Pringle, this is your life. Why does this
always happen to me. I didn't come here to upset you, Mr Spinks.

Spinks Then why did you come here?

Dawn moves back to the window

Dawn I came to warn you.

Spinks Warn me? Everyone seems to be warning me these days.

Dawn Some people are envious. They've worked hard all their lives and have nothing to show for it. And they look at you, and take it personally ...

Spinks And do you know someone like that? Someone who's taking it personally?

Dawn Yes, You're in danger, Mr Spinks. Someone's coming to see you. Someone called Donna Miller. She needs money. She's had all mine — now she wants yours.

Spinks Well, I can always say no, can't I?

Dawn Can you? Men find it difficult to say no to Donna — they find her captivating and exciting. She can be very persuasive.

Spinks Exciting. How will I know this Donna Miller? What does she look like?

Dawn moves close to Spinks until their faces are almost touching

Dawn How well can you see me?

Spinks is aware of Dawn's closeness

Spinks Well enough.

Dawn Then look at me closely. And you'll know Donna when you meet her.

Spinks You're sisters?

Dawn We're twins.

Spinks Identical?

Dawn Yes.

Spinks (*doubtfully*) And you say she's exciting?

Dawn (*smiling*) Oh, she's not like me, Mr Spinks. She's my mirror image — but reflections can be deceptive. Mirrors don't always tell the truth, do they? She's very different from me. Men don't find her boring ...

Spinks You said she was dangerous.

Dawn (*after a pause*) She can be unpredictable ...

Spinks What do you mean, unpredictable?

Dawn I don't want to talk about it.

Spinks You are talking about it.

Dawn I've said enough.

Spinks No, you've either said too little, or too much — you haven't said enough.

Dawn returns to the window

(*Following Dawn*) What's wrong with your sister?

Dawn (*turning*) She has no morals, Mr Spinks.

Spinks (*staring*) No morals? Get away. And you think she'll come here?
Dawn She already has.
Spinks What!
Dawn (*looking out*) Can you see across the road?
Spinks (*looking out*) Just about.
Dawn See the people by the bus stop? See the woman standing slightly apart
— in the short skirt?
Spinks (*staring slightly away from the direction of her gaze*) Yeh.
Dawn That's Donna. She may have followed me. She mustn't find me here.
Is there any other way out?
Spinks There's the back stairs, at the end of the corridor but ——

Dawn moves to the hall door

Wait a minute — are you going?
Dawn I came to warn you — I've warned you. Take care, Mr Spinks.
Spinks Will I see you again?

Dawn stops by the door and looks at him in surprise

Dawn Do you want to see me again?
Spinks Yeah. I don't find you boring. I think you're nice.
Dawn Oh. (*She smiles in confusion*) Thank you.

Dawn exits awkwardly

Spinks returns to the window and peers out. The front door slams

Kingsley puts his head around the kitchen door

Kingsley (*indignantly*) Has she gone?
Spinks Yeh. You've been long enough, Kingsley. What were you doing in
there?
Kingsley Finding things ... (*He comes in, studying a lottery ticket*)

Spinks continues looking out of the window

What did she want?
Spinks She came to warn me — apparently someone's after my money.
Kingsley Oh, yes, the money. This win — was it last Saturday?
Spinks Yeh. The big rollover week. When the church choir from Hull won
it.
Kingsley Oh, yes. And one of the choir had dropped out of the syndicate the
week before they won.

Spinks Yeah, shot himself.
Kingsley Yes. Tragic. Dropped out because he'd been made redundant.
Spinks You'd have thought they'd have given him something.
Kingsley They did — two bottles of white wine, wasn't it?
Spinks Yeah. I thought that was derisory.
Kingsley Still, it meant more for them I suppose — him dropping out. And you did all right.
Spinks Yeah.
Kingsley Who came to see you?
Spinks What?
Kingsley From the Lottery.
Spinks It was a suit.
Kingsley A suit?
Spinks Yeh. Very discreet, very unobtrusive.
Kingsley A suit's not unobtrusive around here. They're all into leisure wear. I'm surprised I didn't spot him.
Spinks You were sleeping it off again.
Kingsley Did he bring the cheque?
Spinks Yeah.
Kingsley That must have been a sight.
Spinks It was.
Kingsley What did you do with it?
Spinks Put it on deposit.
Kingsley Thought you were going to spend it?
Spinks Yeah, in time.
Kingsley In a bloody long time, Spinks.
Spinks What?

Kingsley sits and lays the lottery ticket down in front of Spinks

Kingsley This is your last week's ticket, Spinks. You should have destroyed it.
Spinks You've been searching my kitchen? How dare you search my kitchen.
Kingsley I had a nagging worry that the numbers weren't right. I wasn't sure, but I am now. You can't draw a lottery prize without surrendering the ticket. So what are you up to, Spinks?
Spinks Suppose I said I'd got another ticket.
Kingsley You haven't. You're too mean to buy another ticket. I know you've been lying, Spinks, what I want to know is why?
Spinks (*after a hesitation*) It started off as a joke, really ...
Kingsley I'm not laughing, Spinks. Why?
Spinks (*erupting angrily*) Why! Because I've had that phone for over a fortnight and it hadn't rung once. I'm the man the world forgot, Kingsley

— that's if they ever noticed me in the first place. I'm just some half-blind old git on the tenth floor. I wanted to be someone for a change. Well, the phone's ringing now, isn't it? I'm in the papers. There's even an exciting and unpredictable woman with no morals after me. Things are different now.

Kingsley They will be when they find out. You lied to them, Spinks — they won't like that. What's worse — you lied to me … (*He pours Spinks's whisky back into the bottle*)

Spinks Are you going to tell them?

Kingsley I can't be a party to this. It's deception. I have my reputation to think of.

Spinks What reputation? You haven't got a reputation. You're a piss artist.

Kingsley That's it. We're finished. (*He gets to his feet*)

Spinks (*desperately*) Wait a minute, Kingsley. Listen. What's the next best thing to having money?

Kingsley There's no next best thing.

Spinks There is — it's called credit.

Kingsley Credit?

Spinks We could have credit — we could have standing.

Kingsley We? I see. Now, you haven't got any money you're prepared to share it with me.

Spinks We could be important, Kingsley. Fêted — wined and dined. Life in the fast lane.

Kingsley What makes you think that? You're the one who's supposed to have money. Why should anyone spend money on you? Who'd be that stupid?

Spinks Well, you for a start.

Kingsley (*staring*) What?

Spinks You were going to take me out tonight.

Kingsley Well, yes.

Spinks That's what they'll do. They'll speculate to accumulate.

Kingsley (*frowning*) I didn't do it for that.

Spinks No, of course not.

Kingsley Spinks, they'll expect to see money.

Spinks Why? Millionaires don't carry money. Did the Beatles carry money?

Kingsley Didn't they?

Spinks No. They'd have laughed at the thought.

Kingsley You've thought about this, haven't you?

Spinks I've had a lot of time.

Kingsley It wouldn't last.

Spinks Who cares?

Kingsley I don't know. We're sailing close to the wind here, Spinks.

The phone rings

Spinks (*shrugging*) It's up to you. (*He turns away*)

Kingsley answers the phone

Kingsley (*into the phone*) Hallo? … Yes? Mr Spinks? (*His voice becomes cultured*) I'm speaking on his behalf. As you can imagine he's a little fraught at the moment. … You want him to what? … Oh. In aid of the scanner? … Yes, I do know he has the scanner under serious consideration. … And Help the Aged? I know that's very dear to his heart — after all, he's almost one himself — but he is concerned about overheads. Perhaps we can discuss it further. … Right. We'll wait for you to get back to us. Bye. (*He replaces the phone receiver slowly and looks at Spinks*) My God!
Spinks Who was that?
Kingsley The Round Table. They want you to open the Carnival and judge the Fancy Dress. They want you to come as their guest — they'll send a car.

Kingsley pauses for a moment and then pours the whisky back into Spinks's glass

The Lights fade

The CURTAIN *falls*

SCENE 2

Spinks's flat. A few days later. Eight in the evening

The room is tidier but little else has changed. Various nibbles have been laid out and the table is set for dinner

When the CURTAIN *rises, Kingsley, still in his top coat, is looking around with satisfaction as he drains his glass*

Spinks enters, looking serious and self-conscious in a dark suit

Spinks Well?
Kingsley I like it. That's a very fine piece of serge, Spinks.
Spinks I haven't worn it since the funeral.
Kingsley Don't think about the funeral — don't think about her. This is the night to turn Mother's picture to the wall, Spinks.
Spinks Don't start that.
Kingsley Are you nervous?

Spinks Of course I'm nervous. I've never entertained a woman up here before. (*He hesitates*) And it's been a long time since — you know …
Kingsley How long?
Spinks Long enough.
Kingsley Then you'd better read this.

Kingsley produces a paperback book and hands it to Spinks

I should have given it to you before.
Spinks What is it?
Kingsley "The Perfumed Garden". I swear by it.
Spinks "The Perfumed Garden". I haven't even got a window box.
Kingsley It's not about flowers. It's written by this sheikh. It's a "Song of Sensual Delights and Joyous Imaginings".
Spinks You mean it's a dirty book.
Kingsley No. The sheikh says God wouldn't have given us these desires if he didn't want us to enjoy them.
Spinks I thought we were supposed to resist them. (*He hands the book back*)
Kingsley I hope you're not going to resist them tonight, Spinks. I'm going to a lot of trouble. This book tells you what to look out for. How to recognize when a woman's ready for the supreme moment.
Spinks Get away.
Kingsley Listen. (*He reads*) "She heaves deep sighs, her eyes languish — and her mouth opens as if prior to yawning" … They're the signs — keep an eye out for them. (*He hands the book back to Spinks*)
Spinks "Prior to yawning." Sounds as if she's going to sleep. (*He throws the book down*) I don't need a book on it, Kingsley. I know what it's all about. I've had my moments.
Kingsley (*sharply*) When?
Spinks What?
Kingsley Out of curiosity — when have you had your moments?
Spinks When?
Kingsley Yes.
Spinks First time?
Kingsley First time.
Spinks Bournemouth — one night — under the pier.
Kingsley Under the pier. You call that a moment?
Spinks It had to be — the tide was coming in. (*Pause*) Then there was a night on Dunstable Downs, on an excursion — that was magical. Then somewhere near Greenwich Observatory — that was on a boat trip ——
Kingsley (*staring*) Bournemouth pier — Dunstable Downs — Greenwich Observatory. Spinks, I can't help observing that all these moments of yours seem to have taken place in the open air.

Spinks Well, I couldn't bring them back home. The old lady was strict Anglican.

Kingsley So tonight, if we exclude the pier, will be the first time it's taken place under cover.

Spinks If it takes place.

Kingsley Don't be nervous. Everything's under control. I'm doing you a nice meal. I'm starting with avocado, the well-known aphrodisiac, so potent that the village maidens are locked away during the harvest season.

Spinks I still think she's expecting to go out, Kingsley.

Kingsley You won't get food like this out. I'm doing my speciality. Steak *flambé'*d in brandy.

Spinks Oh no!

Kingsley What's the matter?

Spinks The last time you tried that you lost your eyebrows.

Kingsley Shut up and taste this wine. It's an Australian Chardonnay. Wallaby Creek. Bin 45.

Spinks takes a deep drink

Not too much. That's something I meant to mention. Go easy on the lotion. It'll impair your performance.

Spinks Go easy on the lotion! That's rich coming from you. You're pissed already. I hope you're not going to be hanging about when she's here.

Kingsley Don't worry. I won't let you down. I'll serve the meal and go. Give me credit for a little refinement.

Spinks surveys the table

Spinks Talking of refinement. It's red wine with red meat.

Kingsley (*with a drunken stare*) What?

Spinks It's red wine with red meat.

Kingsley (*after a pause*) The meat won't be red when I've finished with it.

Spinks That's not the point. It's red wine with steak.

Kingsley (*blustering*) I know that! But these stuffy conventions are meant to be broken, aren't they? Or are you some sort of perfectionist, Spinks? I haven't got any red wine.

Spinks (*smugly*) I have. (*He takes a bottle from the sideboard*) An Albanian Burgundy from Christmas. (*He hands the bottle to Kingsley*) Perhaps you could let it breathe for a while …

Kingsley snatches the bottle with a scowl and heads towards the kitchen

Kingsley — what worries me is … Australian Chardonnay — Albanian Burgundy — dining in. I'm supposed to be a millionaire.

Kingsley You're an eccentric millionaire. You haven't got used to your wealth yet.

Spinks But I'm not spending any money.

Kingsley You haven't got any money. But one thing that makes this deception work, Spinks, is that you're a well-known mean bastard. Everyone around here knows that. Just like your father. He always hid in the Gents when it was his round. And he broke his flaming hip trying to find the pisspot in the dark because he was too mean to switch a light on. Am I right or am I wrong?

Spinks (*sighing*) You're right, Kingsley. I do hate spending money.

Kingsley People won't expect you to change overnight.

Spinks But she's not people. This is our first date. She'll expect to go out. I think she'll be suspicious.

Kingsley Let her be suspicious. It's only for tonight. Then you move on, Spinks.

There is the sound of the doorbell

You'd better let her in.

Spinks loosens up with a little sparring, takes a deep breath, and exits into the hall

Kingsley puts the final touches to the table

We hear the voices of Dawn and Spinks, off

Kingsley exits into the kitchen. As he does so, Dawn and Spinks enter

Dawn — who has clearly dressed to go out — stares in surprise at Kingsley's retreating figure

Dawn Oh.

Spinks (*anxiously*) What's the matter?

Dawn What's he doing here?

Spinks He's just doing the meal, that's all.

Dawn The meal? (*She looks round at the table*)

Spinks You expected to go out.

Dawn No, not really, I …

Spinks I thought we could get to know each other better here — but if you want to go out …

Dawn No. It's perfectly all right. (*She looks slowly around the room*)

Spinks What is it?

Dawn You haven't changed anything. Everything's the same. I imagined you'd make changes.

Spinks Yeah, well, I'm not staying here, am I?

Dawn No, I suppose not.

Spinks And the truth is, I find it difficult to let go of the past, know what I mean?

Dawn Yes, I understand that. I find it difficult too. (*She picks up the paperback*) Oh, what are you reading? I always think you can judge a man by the books he reads.

Spinks (*hastily*) It's not mine.

Dawn "The Perfumed Garden". (*She smiles*) Now, we do have something in common.

Spinks (*hopefully*) Do we?

Dawn I have a lovely garden — or I should say, did have. Is there anything on sweet peas?

Spinks takes the book from Dawn

Spinks I haven't read it. I don't read much these days.

Dawn You can get books with large print from the … (*Her voice dies away*) Where are you thinking of moving to? There are some nice properties in Bromley.

Spinks (*importantly*) I am contemplating a move in that direction.

Dawn How sad. Just as I'm moving out. Of course, my little house would be too small for your needs.

Spinks Why are you moving?

Dawn Oh, I feel like a change.

Spinks It's because of your sister, isn't it? Because of the money you gave her.

Dawn Did she get in touch?

Spinks No, and I'd tell her where to go if she did.

Dawn It's not all her fault. There's not much money in teaching the piano these days. I seem to have been overtaken by the electronic organ.

Spinks (*shaking his head*) Technology. It'll be the death of us. Come and sit down …

Dawn takes her coat off and they sit at the table

Wine?

Dawn Thank you. (*She observes the cheap tumblers*)

Spinks (*realizing*) I really must get some decent cut glass. It does enhance a drink, don't you agree?

Dawn Yes, but it doesn't matter.

They drink. There is loud banging from the kitchen

Kingsley (*muffled; off*) Bugger!
Dawn (*anxiously*) What was that?
Spinks Kingsley — he's tenderizing the steak.
Dawn (*with a nervous laugh*) Sounds as if he's tenderizing a few fingers as well. (*She leans forward*) Is he always like this?
Spinks Like what?
Dawn He always seems — drunk.
Spinks He is. He was very big in the Highway Department until the booze got him. White collar job — car allowance — the lot. Worked out your way.

Kingsley enters grinning insanely. He is bearing two plates of avocado

Kingsley The avocado is served. (*He plonks the plates on the table*) Complimented by Wallaby Creek — Bin 45. (*He slops the wine into the glasses*) Bon appetit.

Kingsley sways back into the kitchen

Spinks and Dawn toy with the avocado

Dawn (*whispering*) He's drunk now.
Spinks (*grinning*) You think that's drunk. You should see him —— (*He breaks off*)
Dawn What?
Spinks He's had a tragic life. Lost his wife and family — and his home.
Dawn You mean they're dead?
Spinks No, they kicked him out.
Dawn Why? What happened?
Spinks He won't tell me — just hints, you know. But he was married. (*Pause*) You know, I'm surprised you never tied the knot, Dawn — an attractive girl like you.
Dawn Well, there was someone once.
Spinks I thought so. What was he like?
Dawn Quite handsome. He looked like a young Roger Moore.
Spinks (*disappointed*) Oh.
Dawn I shouldn't have said that — that he was like a young Roger Moore. I've made you jealous.
Spinks (*shrugging*) I'd have been jealous if he'd looked like an old Roger Moore. More wine?
Dawn I don't normally, but I have plunged on a taxi tonight ...

Spinks tops up Dawn's glass. She drinks nervously

Spinks What happened between you and this Roger Moore?
Dawn Something that even now I find difficult to talk about ... (*Emotionally*)
I'm sorry. Where's the little room?
Spinks (*staring*) The little room?
Dawn I need to spend a penny.
Spinks Oh, yeah ... Down the hall — on the right.

Dawn moves towards the hall door

Look, I didn't mean to pry. If I said anything ...

Dawn exits quickly

Kingsley enters with the red wine

Kingsley Where is she?
Spinks Gone for a slash. At least that's what she said. I think I may have upset
her. She became emotional.
Kingsley That's the wine. (*He drinks straight from the bottle*) Things are
going very nicely.
Spinks (*eyeing Kingsley grimly*) Are they?
Kingsley I'm just going to put a match to the steak — it's been marinating.
Spinks It's not the only thing that's been marinating around here. Haven't
you had enough?
Kingsley Don't worry about me — you just do your bit.
Spinks (*nervously*) I don't think she's that sort of girl, Kingsley.
Kingsley Of course she is. They all are. She's like that steak out there — inert
and lifeless at the moment, but once soaked in liquor, all you have to do is
apply the match, and she'll burst into flame. (*He tops up Dawn's glass*)
Spinks Do me a favour, Kingsley. Where do you get this stuff from?
Kingsley Once you've eaten — get her in the bedroom.
Spinks (*alarmed*) I can't do that. Not on the first date.
Kingsley Why not? From what I understand, you never get a second one.
Spinks She won't go through there.
Kingsley She will if she wants your money.
Spinks She didn't come for the money. I told you. She came to warn me
about Donna Miller.
Kingsley Warn you about Donna Miller! Somebody should warn you about
Dawn Pringle. Have you ever seen this Donna Miller?
Spinks Yes, from a distance.
Kingsley You haven't seen anything from a distance in years, Spinks. She
doesn't exist. It was just an excuse. She's hustling you.

Spinks Well, even if she's hustling me — she won't go through there.
Kingsley She will. She just needs a reason — something to cover her modesty. Take her to the window — show her the view. Say the street lights remind you of a string of pearls across the throat of a woman ——
Spinks Hellfire, Kingsley.
Kingsley — then mention that the view is even better from the bedroom ...
Spinks Shut up, Kingsley — for Gawd's sake!

Kingsley moves to the kitchen door and pauses by it

Kingsley And if that doesn't work — arouse her sympathy. Knock a few things over.

Kingsley exits during the following line

Spinks (*angrily*) There's nothing wrong with my ——

Kingsley is gone

Dawn returns looking a little flushed. She sits and glances towards the kitchen

Dawn (*whispering*) Has he gone yet?
Spinks No. He's about to *flambé* the steak.
Dawn Sounds exciting.
Spinks It could be. (*He raises his glass*) Drink up.
Dawn I really shouldn't. I've become quite flushed. (*But she drinks*)
Spinks (*pouring more wine*) I like you flushed. (*He leans forward and touches Dawn's hair*) I've been wanting to do that. It's very smooth — so's your skin ...
Dawn (*shyly*) I'm not very pretty ...
Spinks You feel good.
Dawn I suppose that's important to someone who ...
Spinks What?
Dawn Nothing.
Spinks You don't have to worry — I'm not sensitive about it.
Dawn (*surprised*) You're not?
Spinks (*still with his hand about her hair*) Not with you.
Dawn (*leaning forward*) You know, I have this terrible urge to kiss you.
Spinks (*huskily*) Indulge it.

Dawn moves closer

Dawn (*sniffing*) What's that smell?

Spinks Patchouli oil.
Dawn No. Something's burning!

Smoke drifts in from the kitchen

Kingsley (*shouting; off*) Sod it! Bugger!

Spinks and Dawn stare at each other

Spinks I think we've struck a snag.
Kingsley (*off*) Shit!

> *Kingsley enters, his coat smoking. He rummages in the sideboard and takes a small fire extinguisher from it, then exits at the double*

Spinks and Dawn continue to watch the door. Slowly the pandemonium subsides. Silence

> *Kingsley emerges. He has a smoking tea towel over one arm. Smoke still emanates from his coat. He smiles politely*

Kingsley It's just a thought but I wonder if you'd care for a pizza instead?
Dawn I'm not really hungry.
Spinks Nor am I. That avocado was very filling.
Dawn Yes.

Spinks rises and escorts Kingsley towards the hall

Spinks So, I'll see you in the morning, Kingsley.
Kingsley Well, if you're sure …
Spinks Absolutely.
Kingsley There is cheese and biscuits …
Spinks No, you've done enough. 'Night.

> *Spinks escorts Kingsley out of the hall door*

Dawn crosses to the window and gazes down as if looking for someone

> *Spinks returns and watches Dawn*

Spinks Admiring the view.
Dawn Yes, it's quite breathtaking.

Spinks joins Dawn and looks out

Spinks Yes. (*After a hesitation*) I always think that those lights down there look like strings of pearls across the throat of a woman.

Dawn looks at Spinks in surprise

(*Slyly*) That's what you need, Dawn. They'd set you off.
Dawn Oh, I don't know. I don't think I'm a pearl person …
Spinks You could be. (*Artfully*) That's what I'm looking forward to, now I've got money. Spoiling someone … (*Pause*) Did he spoil you?
Dawn Who?
Spinks This young Roger Moore?
Dawn On the contrary — he was cruel.
Spinks So it wasn't to be?
Dawn Oh, yes — it was to be. At a dance, in the park. He led me away from the other dancers and into the trees.
Spinks (*excitedly*) In the open air?
Dawn Yes. I was so excited. But it was totally humiliating.
Spinks You were seen — that's always a danger.
Dawn He wouldn't have cared if we were. He was drunk. Not that I minded. I wanted him so desperately. It was what he said afterwards …
Spinks What was that?
Dawn He said, "You weren't very good tonight, Donna — I was bored."
Spinks He'd taken you for Donna Miller — Pringle that was.
Dawn That was the only reason he went with me. That's why I was humiliated.
Spinks That's sad. That's one of the saddest things I've heard.
Dawn Please. Don't feel sorry for me. (*She moves away*)

Spinks watches Dawn uncertainly for a moment

Spinks (*the artful look returning*) Why should I feel sorry for you? No-one's ever felt sorry for me … (*He moves and deliberately stumbles against the furniture*)
Dawn (*turning anxiously*) Oh. You've knocked something over, Arthur.
Spinks Have I? I'm always doing that. You'd think I'd know my way round by now.

Dawn studies Spinks sympathetically

Dawn Can't they do anything?
Spinks No, they did a graft but it didn't really take.

Dawn A graft?

Spinks My eyes weren't always this colour — mine were blue. I'm looking at you through a dead man's eyes, Dawn.

Dawn Oh. It's a strange feeling — to think someone is looking at me from beyond the grave.

Spinks It makes a pleasant change for the poor sod — he normally only sees Kingsley.

Dawn leans forward and kisses Spinks lightly; then she sighs deeply

Spinks (*hopefully*) That was almost a yawn.

Dawn I think I'm a little woozy — too much wine.

Spinks Perhaps we'd better take the weight off our feet ...

Dawn What?

Spinks There's a much better view from the bedroom window.

Dawn Is there?

Spinks If you get my drift.

Dawn Yes, I think I get your drift, Arthur.

Spinks (*archly*) Should we go through?

Dawn (*coldly*) What sort of person do you think I am?

Spinks (*after a hesitation*) I don't know. That's what I'm trying to find out.

Dawn Do you think because you've come into money, you can treat me like this?

Spinks (*alarmed*) No.

Dawn I'm disappointed in you, Arthur. They say money changes people. Well, it certainly hasn't taken long in your case, has it? (*She picks up her coat*)

Spinks I'm sorry. There's been a misunderstanding. I thought you knew what you were in for.

Dawn If I'd known what I was in for, as you so delicately put it, I wouldn't have come.

Spinks (*unhappily*) Look, I think we've got off on the wrong foot. You see, I thought ——

Dawn I know what you thought. I'm afraid you were mistaken in me — but what I find even more heartbreaking, I was mistaken in you, Arthur.

Dawn exits angrily

Spinks sinks miserably into a chair. He looks at his hands; they are shaking. He sits for a few moments. He mops his face with his handkerchief

Kingsley enters quietly and watches Spinks

Spinks looks up

Spinks (*bitterly*) What have you come for? Don't tell me you've brought the
   After Eight mints.
Kingsley I was outside. She didn't stay long. What happened?
Spinks It was a disaster. You and "She heaves deep sighs and her eyes
   languish". You and, "Put a match to her and she'll burst into flame". You
   and, "There's a better view from the bedroom".
Kingsley It didn't work?
Spinks Of course it didn't — because that wasn't me talking, that was you!
Kingsley Well, don't worry about it. There'll be others. Find 'em, fuck 'em,
   and forget 'em, Spinks.
Spinks (*erupting*) Don't use that word in here!

Kingsley backs away

   You still don't get it. You don't understand women, Kingsley. Why do you
   always make it sound like rape? Doesn't the word love ever enter your
   vocabulary?
Kingsley (*staring*) Love.
Spinks I wanted a friend.
Kingsley I'm your friend.
Spinks A girlfriend. Someone to get a card from at Christmas. Someone to
   buy a present for on her birthday. Someone to share things with — if it's
   only a pizza. Someone to ring you late at night ——

The phone rings. They stare at each other

Kingsley You see. She's regretted it already. She's thought about the money.
   Don't be too eager.

Spinks answers the phone

Spinks (*into the phone*) Hallo? … Yeah. … Oh, it's you. … What? …
   When? …I don't know about that. I'll have to see. (*He puts the phone
   down thoughtfully*)
Kingsley You're learning, Spinks. I knew she'd come round. Now, who
   doesn't understand women?
Spinks You don't. That was Donna Miller. The woman who doesn't
   exist …

The Lights fade

The Curtain *falls*

Spinks's flat. Two days later. Early afternoon

When the CURTAIN *rises, Kingsley is sitting reading one of a number of brochures and sipping from a vodka bottle*

Spinks enters. He is wearing an overcoat and gloves. He regards Kingsley for a moment and turns back to the hall

Kingsley Where are you going?

Spinks Thought I'd just check the number on the door — see if it's my flat.

Kingsley I couldn't stay down there, Spinks. He was playing the Sabre Dance again.

Spinks moves to the teapot and lifts the lid

Spinks Want a cuppa?

Kingsley Not on top of vodka, you know I never mix my drinks.

Spinks replaces the lid and moves to the window

Where's Goody Two-shoes?

Spinks Do you mean Dawn?

Kingsley Yes.

Spinks She's got the humpties and gone home.

Kingsley She's not still mad about the other night?

Spinks No, she says she's forgiven me.

Kingsley Well, that's big of her I must say. You were only paying her a compliment. You made a mistake there, Spinks. Where women are concerned, never explain and never apologize. They consider it a sign of weakness. Where have you been?

Spinks Where do you think? Feeding the ducks. That's all I can afford these days — and I tell you this, I begrudge them the bread.

Kingsley Women are an expensive luxury, Spinks.

Spinks You're telling me.

Kingsley Things aren't working out then?

Spinks She's beginning to wonder, Kingsley. Where are the trappings of wealth?

Kingsley I told you what to say. That all your money's on the money market at three months' notice while your advisers prepare an attractive portfolio.

Spinks I've told her that but it doesn't carry much conviction with gloves like these. (*He holds up a gloved hand to reveal a thumb sticking out of the leather*) My thumb's poking out. I couldn't even wave goodbye — I had to give her the clenched fist salute!

Kingsley (*after a pause*) I know where we could get money …
Spinks Where?
Kingsley I know how we could raise a hundred thousand.
Spinks How?
Kingsley It would mean sacrifice …
Spinks I don't mind sacrifice. I'm desperate.

Kingsley hands Spinks a brochure

Kingsley I insure your life for a hundred thousand.
Spinks Yeah?
Kingsley Then we go to Brighton for the day. Right?
Spinks Right.
Kingsley You go in for a dip.
Spinks Yeah.
Kingsley We never see you again.
Spinks What?
Kingsley They find your clothes in a neat pile on the beach. You've drowned, Spinks.
Spinks That's what I call sacrifice.
Kingsley You've drowned but you've made a hundred thousand pounds.
Spinks No, you've made a hundred thousand pounds — I've drowned.
Kingsley No. The assumption is you've drowned. You surface in Tangier.
Spinks That's a long way to swim under water, Kingsley. And while I'm surfacing in Tangier, what are you doing?
Kingsley I'm collecting the money. But I'm grief-stricken. I need a holiday. Where do I go?
Spinks Tangier.
Kingsley Right. I'm walking through the kasbah — who do I see? A familiar figure. Arthur Spinks — now known as Walter Bryce, a name taken from a gravestone in Wapping, with a passport to match.
Spinks And what about Dawn? Is she going to surface in Tangier?
Kingsley No, you couldn't trust a woman with a secret like that. You'd have to make do with a belly dancer.
Spinks I've got a better idea. I'll insure your life for a hundred thousand — and you surface in Tangier.

Spinks hands the brochure back to Kingsley

Kingsley (*sadly*) Who'd insure me, in my state of health? I mean, look at me.
Spinks (*sympathetically*) What is wrong with you?
Kingsley (*after a pause*) They did tell me but I've forgotten what it was. I couldn't pronounce it. I couldn't spell it. I'm dying of something I can't pronounce and I can't spell. I think it has an x in it, or was it a q?

Spinks A q. It wasn't tequila, was it? You're drinking too much.

Kingsley It's the only thing that keeps me sane. (*He regards Spinks curiously*) Are you serious about this woman, Spinks?

Spinks This woman. Do you mean Dawn?

Kingsley Are you?

Spinks (*guardedly*) I might be.

Kingsley It won't last.

Spinks How do you know?

Kingsley Nothing lasts. Love's like a jar of mustard—you never think you'll get to the bottom of it, but you always do.

Spinks God! You're bitter. What happened to make you so cynical, Kingsley? I often wonder what strange tide washed you up here. Perhaps they found your clothes in a neat pile somewhere.

Kingsley I notice she never asks you back to her place.

Spinks She lives out at Bromley, doesn't she? It's a long way. Besides, she's got the decorators in — she's trying to sell it.

Kingsley They sound like excuses to me.

Spinks Look, you can't blame her for being careful. A woman on her own has to be wary of live-in lovers.

Kingsley (*amused*) Live-in what?

Spinks (*defiantly*) Lovers.

Kingsley But you're a long way from being a live-in lover, aren't you, Spinks? A long way ...

Spinks Yeah, well, she wants to be sure of her feelings, doesn't she? And she's religious — she belongs to this church.

Kingsley What sort of church?

Spinks Well, it's a sort of offshoot of the Anabaptists and Primitive Methodists, with leanings towards spiritualism, and a nodding acquaintance with Christian Science. It's called the Church of the New Faithful.

Kingsley So what we have here is a sect, Spinks?

Spinks I suppose so. It was very big in Bromley once. And there were tens of thousands worldwide.

Kingsley How many are there now?

Spinks Worldwide?

Kingsley Yes.

Spinks Fifteen.

Kingsley Fifteen!

Spinks Well, it's a very exacting religion.

Kingsley What do they believe in?

Spinks It's what they don't believe in, really. They don't believe in Christmas, birthdays, Sunday opening, strong drink, modern medicine, and anything cooked in a microwave — that's fairly new.

Kingsley What do they do when they're sick?

Spinks Laying on of hands.

Kingsley No wonder their numbers have dwindled. And what about sex?

Spinks (*after a hesitation*) Sex?

Kingsley Yes.

Spinks Not before marriage — and for that you need permission of the elders.

Kingsley Another reason why their numbers have dwindled. (*Pause*) You're thinking of marrying her, aren't you?

Spinks I might be.

Kingsley You're making a big mistake. She's frigid — religion's just a cloak.

Spinks You don't know that.

Kingsley You'd be better off with her sister.

Spinks Why?

Kingsley Didn't you say she had no morals?

Spinks (*indignantly*) That doesn't mean I'd be better off with her. What sort of person do you think I am? I've got standards, Kingsley, even if you haven't.

Kingsley Has this Donna Miller rung again?

Spinks No, and I don't want her to. The last thing I want to be involved in is a *ménage à trois*.

Kingsley (*grinning*) A what?

Spinks A *ménage à trois*. It's French.

Kingsley I know it's French.

Spinks It means a menagerie of three.

Kingsley Are you sure?

Spinks Of course I'm sure.

Kingsley And what's going to happen when you tell them you haven't got any money, Spinks? I'll tell you — you'll be in a menagerie of one.

Spinks Perhaps it won't make any difference with Dawn. She's attracted to me — she said so.

Kingsley Don't you believe it. Do you know what really attracts women? Money and power. Read your "Perfumed Garden". Know what the old sheikh said? "If a man's not strong or rich he can obtain nothing from a woman."

Spinks That's your cynical attitude again, Kingsley.

Kingsley (*slyly*) Has she advised you to make a will yet?

Spinks gives Kingsley a sharp glance

Spinks What?

Kingsley She has, hasn't she?

Spinks What makes you think that?

Kingsley Because that's what wives usually do. They like to think you're providing for them, even when you're dead.

Spinks (*after a hesitation*) She said it would be the sensible thing to do.
Kingsley And did she suggest who the main beneficiary might be?
Spinks No, she's not interested.
Kingsley Interested enough to mention it. Don't do it, Spinks.
Spinks It doesn't matter, Kingsley, because there isn't any money anyway.
Kingsley But she doesn't know that. You're ten floors up — your eyesight's bad — and you're punchy. There could be an accident: "Unsteady on his feet — too close to those railings — didn't see the edge — tripped." They could be scraping you off that forecourt like strawberry jam — no questions asked.
Spinks Well, the joke would be on her, wouldn't it? Because there isn't any money.
Kingsley (*staring*) Would you say that again? I don't think I heard you properly. You're spread out down there like strawberry jam, and the joke's on her! You're not making sense. You've not made sense since you met her.
Spinks I don't want to talk about it.
Kingsley Spinks, we've got a good thing going here. We've been invited to the mayor's open evening — all we can eat and drink on the rates. We've got a free weekend in Spain to look at that villa. There's a wine tasting at the Holiday Inn — and a demonstration trip in a Rolls-Royce — and all in the next few days. And you prefer to feed the ducks with Miss Frigid Arse.
Spinks (*angrily*) That's enough, Kingsley.
Kingsley She's as cold as a witch's tit and you know it.

Spinks raises his hands and crouches slightly. For a brief moment he reveals the lethal menace of a professional boxer

Spinks Kingsley, if you say one more word against her, I swear I'll drop you.
Kingsley I see. So it's violence now, is it? That's what it's come to. Violence between you and me. That's what she's done to us.

Kingsley exits into the hall

Spinks (*calling after Kingsley*) Kingsley!

Spinks heads towards the hall door to follow Kingsley

The voices of Kingsley and Donna are heard, off. The front door slams

Donna Miller enters. She is the mirror image of Dawn, but with her hair loose. She is wearing a plain, simple mac and is carrying a shoulder bag

Spinks fails to recognize that this is not Dawn

Donna He was in a hurry.

Spinks (*delightedly*) I thought you'd gone home. Look, I'm sorry about lunchtime. It was my fault. You see, I don't eat lunch. I never thought. I know a bag of plums wasn't really the thing …

Spinks kisses Donna. Donna looks mildly surprised. Spinks finds the kiss surprisingly enjoyable

You've changed your perfume. Nice. Don't worry. I'm not going to start on that subject again. I know we've got to give it time — get to know each other before we do it. But I sometimes think we'd get to know each other quicker if we did it first … (*He kisses her again. He finds it encouraging*) I think you've changed. You seem different. Even your kisses are different … You … My God … (*He stands back, appalled*) It's not you, is it?

Donna Isn't it? I thought it was.

Spinks You're Donna Miller — Donna Pringle that was. (*He stares at her*)

Donna (*returning his stare with a level gaze*) Yes.

Spinks What have I done?

Donna (*smiling*) Well, not my sister, by the sound of it.

Donna removes her mac and throws it on a chair. The difference between Donna and Dawn is now more marked: the top buttons on her shirt are undone, her skirt is shorter, her make-up more elaborate, her posture more challenging. She surveys the room

So this is where you live?

Spinks Yeah.

Donna I thought you'd come into money?

Spinks I have.

Donna Well, you're certainly keeping it a secret.

Spinks I'll be leaving here soon, don't you worry. Soon as I get things sorted. I'll be getting rid of all this stuff.

Donna Have you informed Sotheby's?

Spinks What?

Donna The ship's wheel that lights up is definitely a collector's item.

Spinks That has sentimental value. As I told your sister, I find it difficult to let go of the past.

Donna Well, when you finally do let go — where are you going to live?

During the following speech, Donna watches Spinks with a sardonic smile

Spinks (*loftily*) Somewhere in the country. A gentleman's residence — not too grand, but with all the usual amenities. Tennis court — hard of course.

Heated swimming pool — preferably indoors, otherwise you find it full of
frogs; probably have it situated in the stable block. (*He looks at her to see
the effect of his words*)
Donna Stable block? Chase me! (*She sits*)
Spinks Why did you come here?
Donna I wanted to meet the man my sister wants to marry. I wanted to know
if his intentions are honourable, or if he's trifling with her.
Spinks I'm not trifling. I haven't had the chance.
Donna She's been hurt before.
Spinks I know that.
Donna You know she's almost a virgin, don't you?
Spinks You can't be almost a virgin.
Donna She can. Men have visited the moon more often than my sister. That's
why I wanted to meet you.
Spinks Well, now you've met me. I suppose you wonder what she sees in
me. Is it my personal charm, or do I use chloroform?
Donna Why do you say that?
Spinks Well, Kingsley says there's only one thing to do with a face like mine
and that's cover the mirrors.
Donna Who's Kingsley?
Spinks The bloke who just left.
Donna I think I know him from somewhere.
Spinks He came from your way. Worked for the Council. Very big in the
Highways Department until the booze got him. He says Dawn's after my
money.
Donna She's never been interested in money. (*Pause*) What do you think?
Spinks Well, women have never shown any interest in me before.

Donna studies Spinks

Donna That's because you've probably, only recently, grown into your
looks.
Spinks (*staring*) Grown into my looks? What does that mean?
Donna There's a time in everyone's life when they grow into their looks.
When everything comes together — and they look at their best. It can
happen at any age — when you're young, even when you're old. I think
that's happened to you. I think you're at your best, Spinks.
Spinks (*sheepishly*) Get out of it.
Donna No. I can see what attracted her. In fact, I sensed that attraction just
now.
Spinks Did you? (*Pause*) Can I get you a drink?

Donna looks around

Donna Vodka'll do.

Spinks pours a drop of vodka into a glass

Spinks Anything with it?
Donna Yes. Vodka.
Spinks (*grinning*) A woman after my own heart. (*He fills up Donna's glass and the pours one for himself. He studies her*)
Donna What are you looking at?
Spinks I can't get over the likeness. She said you were like a reflection.
Donna I'm no-one's reflection. I'm the original. I was born first. And I've been first ever since. (*She leans back and crosses her legs*)

Spinks watches Donna and then drags his eyes away

Spinks If it wasn't for the make-up and the hair — and the … (*Back to the legs again*) Of course, Dawn doesn't wear much make-up.
Donna No, she thinks it's a snare — it's against her religious principles.
Spinks You're not like that then?
Donna I don't believe in organized religion. I believe in the individual. I believe my body's a church — and we're all free to worship as we wish. (*She uncrosses her legs*)
Spinks I've never heard it put like that before. You're certainly not like your sister.
Donna You know my sister's trouble? She's too serious — no sense of humour. She wouldn't see a joke, except by appointment, and then she'd be late.
Spinks You shouldn't talk about your sister like that.
Donna I can talk about her like that, because she is my sister. I wouldn't let anyone else talk about her. (*Pause*) What does she say about me?
Spinks She said you'd had all her money and now you were after mine.
Donna (*sighing*) She will dramatize things. I was coming to you with a simple business proposition. (*She crosses her legs again*)

Spinks finds himself staring

Spinks How simple?
Donna The opportunity to invest in a dress shop — an investment that could yield instant dividends …

Spinks's gaze returns to Donna's legs

Spinks What dress shop's this, then?

Donna It's in Newbury. Millennium Fashions. Millennium — that was a
shade optimistic; we'll be lucky to last the month.
Spinks Where did you go wrong?
Donna I didn't. It's a question of business confidence — with the right sort
of money behind us …
Spinks (*doubtfully*) I don't know about a dress shop — sounds risky.

*Donna stands and moves around the room during the following. Spinks is
aware of her feline grace*

Donna You wouldn't be investing in a dress shop — you'd be investing in
me. You don't invest in things — you invest in people, Spinks. I have flair
— I have a sense of colour — I have style. (*She turns like a tigress*) I have
energy and drive. I didn't fail in Newbury — Newbury failed me.
Spinks (*clearing his throat*) The trouble is, my money's tied up at the
moment …

Donna gives Spinks a cold stare

Donna Oh. I see. It appears I'm wasting my time. (*She reaches for her coat*)
Spinks Wait a minute. At least finish your drink.

Donna hesitates, then sits and takes up her drink

May I ask you a personal question?
Donna Yes.
Spinks Are you wearing stockings?
Donna Why do you ask?
Spinks They must be very sheer …
Donna They are extremely sheer.
Spinks You normally hear them rasp …
Donna No, they don't rasp — not of this quality. Although I don't really need
to wear them — my legs are quite tanned. And sometimes I don't. After all,
there's nothing smoother than skin …
Spinks No.

They regard her legs for a moment

What did you mean just now, when you said you sensed the attraction?
Donna (*smiling*) Oh, that. Well, Dawn and I may be different in almost every
respect — but we do share some things …
Spinks What things?
Donna A weakness for the same men.

Spinks Get away.

Donna We're twins. Mother always dressed us the same. Our clothes,
presents were always identical. One never had a thing the other didn't have
— and, if it ever did occur — what one had the other wanted ...

Spinks Like the young Roger Moore?

Donna She told you? I can't hurt her like that again ... (*She rises and bends
over Spinks and kisses him slowly on the lips*) Goodbye, Spinks. (*She picks
up her mac and moves to the door*)

Spinks (*hastily*) Wait a minute. I was listening to the Chancellor on *The
World at One*. He was very optimistic about the economy.

Donna Was he?

Spinks Yeah. He anticipated an upturn which he thinks will be consumer-
led — with an increase in High Street spending ... Perhaps the time's ripe
for a judicious investment in a dress shop ...

*Donna smiles. She returns to the centre of the room. She throws her mac back
on the chair. She looks down at Spinks and slowly begins to remove her ear-
rings*

The Lights fade

The CURTAIN *falls*

ACT II
SCENE 1

Spinks's flat. Sunday afternoon

The room has become crowded with goods on approval and "freebies"

When the CURTAIN *rises, Spinks is sitting at the table in his best suit. He is studying a legal document*

Kingsley enters carrying a full pint of beer

Kingsley (*dramatically*) I carried this all the way from the *Jockey* without spilling it.
Spinks I'm more impressed you carried it all the way without drinking it.

Kingsley takes the top off the pint and then reaches into his pocket and takes out a small bottle of vodka. He adds this to the beer. Spinks watches him sourly

You must be spending a fortune in there.
Kingsley I'm not — you are. It's on your slate.
Spinks What!
Kingsley Don't worry — your credit's still good. (*He eyes the various goods*) What's all this?
Spinks Goods on approval — promotional gifts and bribes. It seems everyone wants to be assured of my future custom.
Kingsley You were right, Spinks. Credit is the next best thing to money. (*He regards Spinks's best suit*) Where have you been? I waited two hours in there.
Spinks (*sighing*) I suppose I may as well get it over with. I'll tell you just once — and I don't want any comments.
Kingsley Right. (*Pause*) Well, where have you been?
Spinks Church.
Kingsley (*scornfully*) Church?
Spinks (*sharply*) That was a comment.
Kingsley If there was a certain inflection in my voice — it was from disappointment, because your mother has won at last. She raised you in superstitious bigotry and empty ritual and why? To make you blindly

obedient and unquestioning. Most of the misery in the world springs from religion — it's the weapon of the fanatic, Spinks.

Spinks stares at Kingsley for a moment

Spinks You said all that with an inflection? Well, I'm glad you didn't make a comment — we'd have been here all day. It's not my fault you've lost your faith. Church would do you good, Kingsley.

Kingsley You don't believe all that crap, surely?

Spinks (*shrugging*) I'm an old church boy — I can't change now.

Kingsley But it's not your church, is it?

Spinks (*after a hesitation*) No. They've got a room over the Co-op.

Kingsley Over the Co-op! What are they doing over the Co-op?

Spinks They've opened a mission here. They're worried about the decline in morals — particularly with regard to drink.

Kingsley frowns

I know it's not much of a place. But Brother Jonathan — he's the elder — he has hopes of a revival.

Kingsley (*sitting at the table*) And does he prophesy that a prince will come of great wealth but clad in simple raiment and make then a power in the land?

Spinks What are you talking about?

Kingsley I'm talking about you. It's a shake-down, Spinks. She's not going to ask you for the money. Brother Jonathan is. They'll share it between them.

Spinks Aren't you forgetting something? I haven't got any money.

Kingsley stares at him for a moment

Kingsley I keep forgetting that. (*Pause*) And how do you reconcile this new interest in religion with Donna Miller?

Spinks (*alarmed*) Keep your voice down. She'll be back in a minute.

Kingsley Who will?

Spinks Dawn — she's getting a few things for Sunday lunch,

Kingsley (*staring*) I do Sunday lunch.

Spinks Well, she's doing it today. After all, it lessens the fire risk, Kingsley.

Kingsley I'll repeat my question. How do you reconcile all this with Donna Miller?

Spinks I can't. I'm tormented with guilt.

Kingsley Has she been round here again?

Spinks (*after a hesitation*) Yes.

Kingsley What's going on, Spinks?

Spinks (*archly*) Read your "Perfumed Garden". "A man who deserves favours of a woman does not boast of her acquaintance."

Kingsley So that's it! You bugger, Spinks!

Spinks I couldn't resist her. She was laid out there like lamb and lettuce, Kingsley.

Kingsley She's not like her sister then?

Spinks No. Donna doesn't believe in organized religion. She believes in the individual. She says her body's a church.

Kingsley If it is — they've turned it into a supermarket. Shame on you, Spinks.

Spinks I can't help myself. She appeals to the dark side of my nature. She only has to remove her ear-rings.

Kingsley Does she? You're getting in very deep, Spinks.

Spinks They're like two sides of the same coin. One good, one bad.

Kingsley You could be in trouble.

Spinks I am. (*Pause*) I've given Donna a cheque, Kingsley.

Kingsley What!

Spinks Post-dated.

Kingsley Never mind about it being post-dated. How much?

Spinks Fifty thousand.

Kingsley Bloody hell! When is it due?

Spinks End of the month. It was to keep her creditors at bay.

Kingsley And what happens when she tries to present it? Who's going to keep her at bay?

Spinks I hadn't thought that far ahead.

Kingsley And what about her creditors? There's a law against issuing cheques with insufficient funds. You're going to get your collar felt, Spinks.

Spinks I thought I could stop the cheque later.

Kingsley That won't make any difference. She'll have the cheque — and that's evidence. Evidence that you had knowledge of a woman under false pretences.

Spinks (*after a pause*) It isn't like a gambling debt, then?

Kingsley No, it's not like a gambling debt. You're in deep shit, Spinks.

Spinks I thought I might be. I'm running out of control, Kingsley. I'm going down the gradient at high speed with the throttle open and the lights at red. And when I look at Dawn's sweet, trusting face, I feel ashamed. I never meant it to happen, I swear. I never expected to be involved in an eternal triangle — not at my time of life.

Kingsley It won't be eternal — not when Dawn finds out.

Spinks I know. She's had one bad experience — and I'm doing it to her again. I'm afraid it'll tip her over the edge, Kingsley.

Kingsley (*darkly*) She's already over the edge.

Spinks What do you mean?

Kingsley She may be a talented musician but I think she's one black note short of a keyboard.

Spinks Don't start on her. She doesn't approve of you as it is.

Kingsley I know how she feels about me. And I know I'm not welcome at this table. I'll go. (*He rises*)

Spinks Before you go. Sign this. (*He pushes the document forward, partly covering it with his hand, and hands Kingsley a pen*)

Kingsley What is it?

Spinks Just witness my signature. Where the geezer across the landing's signed …

Kingsley moves Spinks's hand

Kingsley This is a will.

Spinks Yeah.

Kingsley So she's persuaded you to make one, after all I said.

Spinks She merely pointed out the danger of not making a will.

Kingsley What danger?

Spinks The danger that some unworthy person may turn up and inherit the whole estate.

Kingsley What unworthy person?

Spinks A relative.

Kingsley You haven't got any relatives.

Spinks Of course I've got relatives. I wasn't made up from a kit.

Kingsley All right. You may have relatives but you haven't got an estate.

Spinks Well, I haven't got fifty thousand pounds but I made a cheque out for it.

Kingsley I see. And now you're going to do the same for Dawn. Donna gets fifty thousand of nothing — and Dawn gets a residue of nothing. At least you're fair, Spinks. Or do you think this will earn you a little gratitude without costing you anything … ?

Spinks (*guiltily*) The thought never occurred to me.

Kingsley I bet it didn't. So she pointed out the danger of not making a will. What about the danger of making a will? I don't have to look to know who the main beneficiary is.

Spinks It's the least I can do.

Kingsley I don't suppose I even get a mention.

Spinks You get five thousand pounds, on the condition you book into a clinic.

Kingsley Well, that's something I suppose —— (*he breaks off*) I'm doing it again! There isn't any money, Spinks.

Spinks She doesn't know that.

Kingsley Right. And when I sign this I could be signing your death warrant.

Spinks Just sign it, Kingsley. I trust her, all right?

Kingsley Well, don't go on the balcony with her.

Spinks I seem to remember it was you who wanted to insure my life for a hundred grand. Perhaps I shouldn't go on the balcony with you.

Kingsley If that's how you feel, then I'm happy to sign. And I wish you joy. (*He signs the will with a flourish*)

Spinks We can trust her, Kingsley. She's as honest as the day is long.

Kingsley (*darkly*) But the nights are drawing in, Spinks — especially for you.

Spinks It's not the money with her — I know it isn't.

Kingsley Prove it.

Spinks I will.

Kingsley The only way you can prove it, is to tell her the truth — and you won't do that, will you … ?

Kingsley exits

The front door slams

Spinks tries discarding the will in various parts of the room, doing his best to make its appearance prominent but casual. Finally he leaves it on a chair

There is the sound of the front door opening

Dawn enters with shopping

Dawn I waited until he'd gone. I saw him crossing the road with a pint of beer. He really lowers the tone.

Spinks Well, he's gone now.

Dawn He'll be back.

Dawn clears the table during the following. She moves the will from the chair to the sideboard without a glance. Spinks looks disappointed

Did you enjoy the service, Arthur?

Spinks Well, it wasn't what I've been used to …

Dawn Brother Jonathan took to you straight away.

Spinks What makes you think that?

Dawn He gave you a kiss of peace — he doesn't do that to everyone. He said, he saw you in a golden light, Arthur.

Spinks What does that mean?

Dawn It's an aura. He's very strong on auras.

Spinks (*unimpressed*) Is he?

Dawn What's the matter? Didn't you like him?

Spinks To tell the truth, Dawn, I thought he was on the scrounge.

Dawn On the scrounge! Really, Arthur — having money's made you so suspicious. (*She moves the will aside to put down her shopping*)

Again Spinks is disappointed

Spinks He kept talking about the day when they'd be raised up and wax fat and fruitful in the land of the ungodly — and he kept looking at me. I just wondered who was expected to do the raising up.

Dawn Not you, that's obvious — not after the collection. Everyone saw the fifty p go in.

Spinks Well, I didn't want to indulge in a display of undue ostentation — not on my first visit.

Dawn You certainly didn't. We shan't get Brother Robert a new car that way.

Spinks I don't see why he needs a new car.

Dawn He needs a new car for his pastoral duties.

Spinks There was only seven in the congregation.

Dawn They happen to live far apart.

Spinks Well, he doesn't need top of the range. He showed me the brochure. I've never seen so many extras. Power assisted steering — central locking — collapsible column — airbags ——

Dawn We want him to be safe. We can't afford to lose him — there are only seven of us. Suppose he had a fatal accident.

Spinks Well, wouldn't that be a sign that God wanted to see him?

Dawn If you're going to be facetious, Arthur.

Spinks I'm sorry, Dawn. I suppose I've always had this frugal nature.

Dawn Frugal. You and Kingsley were test driving a Rolls-Royce the other day.

During the following, Dawn sees the will, picks it up and studies it with mounting incredulity

Spinks We didn't drive it. We sat in the back, because I couldn't see and he couldn't stand. It would mean a chauffeur. That's what happens when you start spending money — one thing leads to another. It also means it's going to stand out there being covered in envy scratches. I think we shall have to wait until we move out. Now Kingsley's talking about a Ferrari with wire wheels and personalized number plates. To tell the truth, I'm finding it all rather a strain. (*He looks up and sees Dawn studying the will*)

Dawn Arthur, this is your will.

Spinks (*in great surprise*) Is it? So that's where it got to. I thought I'd put it away. I didn't mean you to see that.

Dawn Arthur, you can't do this.

Spinks You said I should make a will.

Dawn But it appears that I'm the main beneficiary.

Spinks Well, why not?

Dawn Arthur, when I advised you to make a will — I wasn't thinking of myself. This makes me feel awful.

Spinks You'll get used to it — I did. You'll be a rich woman one day, Dawn. (*He studies her*) A very rich woman — if anything happens to me.

Dawn But I don't want anything to happen to you. I don't want to be a rich woman — the truth is, money's always frightened me.

Spinks You're right to be frightened. It can be a curse, Dawn.

Dawn You don't have to leave it to me. There are plenty of good causes. Help the Aged — Save the Children — Oxfam — Christian Aid — Action Aid — Amnesty International — The Lifeboats — RSPCA — NSPCC — Scope — Sense — Red Cross — Madam Curie — Mother Teresa — Bosnia — Bangladesh — Ethiopia … (*She pauses for breath*)

Spinks What about the Kurds?

Dawn (*staring*) The Kurds?

Spinks Nothing against the Kurds, have you?

Dawn No, I simply hadn't thought about them.

Spinks A much-abused minority. Still, it's your decision. If you want to give it to charity, that's up to you. Because you're going to be a rich woman one day — very rich.

Dawn But you hardly know me, Arthur.

Spinks Whose fault's that?

Dawn What?

Spinks Don't get me wrong. I just want to see you right, that's all. When I'm gone — and after all, I'm older than you are — you'll be a very rich woman — very rich.

Dawn You're not old, Arthur.

Spinks Well, I'm feeling it at the moment. I think I'll get a breath of air … I get giddy sometimes … (*He moves to the balcony and steps out*)

Dawn continues to study the will

(*Glancing over his shoulder*) Now, put that in a safe place, Dawn. We don't want any dispute in the family if anything should happen to me — because you're going to be a very rich woman — very rich …

Dawn folds the will neatly and puts it in the drawer of the sideboard. She turns and watches Spinks silently. Spinks leans over the balcony railings. Dawn walks silently across the room towards him. Her face is expressionless

(*Leaning further over*) There's Kingsley threading his way through the traffic.

Dawn stands behind him

They'll get him one day — that's for sure.

Dawn stretches out a hand and places it on Spinks's shoulder. He turns abruptly, his hands clenching the railings. Their eyes meet for a moment

Dawn Arthur, don't lean over the edge like that — you could fall.
Spinks Don't worry — I had a firm grip on the rail. No. But you're right — it's not safe out here.

Spinks comes back into the room. Dawn returns to the dresser and takes out the will. She crumples it into a ball and throws it into the bin

Spinks (*staring*) What are you doing?
Dawn I can't take it. It would be blood money. I won't gain by your death. Give it to Kingsley.
Spinks (*relieved*) You don't know how much I'd like to tell him that. (*He puts his arms around Dawn*)
Dawn I couldn't live without you, Arthur. If anything happened to you — I'd kill myself.
Spinks Don't say that. I'm not worth it.
Dawn You are to me. You're the only person who's ever been kind and gentle, and patient …
Spinks But you hardly know me.
Dawn But I want to. I want to know everything about you, Arthur. No secrets.
Spinks (*guardedly*) Do you?
Dawn You don't confide easily, do you, Arthur? I mean, you're very close.
Spinks I suppose I am. I suppose that's why I never had any friends. They got tired of telling me all their secrets and me telling them sod all — not that there was anything to tell — until now …

They kiss

Dawn If my sister could see me now.
Spinks (*uneasily*) Yeh.
Dawn (*after a pause*) She hasn't been here, has she?
Spinks Been here? No. What made you say that?
Dawn Well, she did say she was going to call.

Spinks What does she say now?

Dawn She never mentions you.

Spinks Probably thought better of it.

Dawn Yes … (*Pause*) I know it's silly but sometimes I think I can smell her perfume …

Spinks Her perfume? No. I know what that is. My financial consultant came yesterday.

Dawn Your financial consultant's a woman?

Spinks Yeah. Very smart — business-like.

Dawn Is she attractive?

Spinks Sort of.

Dawn Now I'm jealous.

Spinks No, it's strictly business, Dawn.

Dawn regards Spinks in silence for a moment

Dawn Do you mind waiting for lunch, Arthur?

Spinks Why?

Dawn I'd like to see that view from the other window …

Spinks (*staring*) In the bedroom?

Dawn Yes …

Spinks Well, it's just the same as this —— (*he breaks off*) Dawn!

Dawn Don't expect too much. I sometimes feel it's a dance I've never quite learned the steps to.

Spinks Don't worry — I'll lead.

Spinks picks Dawn up in his arms

Dawn You're so confident, Arthur.

Spinks You know why, Dawn? You've given me back my self-esteem. Something I thought I'd lost for ever …

Spinks staggers back a step and they crash into the furniture

Dawn I could walk, Arthur.

Spinks You're not walking. I'm carrying you.

Dawn My gentle giant.

Spinks sways short-sightedly across the room. They collide with more furniture

Arthur, are you sure this is a good idea?

They crash into the doorpost

Oh dear, I hope this isn't going to end in anti-climax.
Spinks Don't worry, darling. It won't …

Spinks exits with Dawn

There is a heavy crash, off

The Lights fade

The CURTAIN *falls*

SCENE 2

Spinks's flat. The following Sunday afternoon

When the CURTAIN *rises Kingsley is sitting by the electric fire in his topcoat reading a book, a glass in his hand*

Spinks enters in his Sunday best. His tie is awry and he looks a little dishevelled. His hand is grazed

Kingsley eyes Spinks curiously

Spinks You still here?
Kingsley Just getting a warm, Spinks. You don't begrudge me that, surely.
Spinks Well, just go down to one bar, will you? (*He moves to the sideboard and glances into the teapot*) Want a cuppa?
Kingsley No. (*He glances at Spinks's hand*) What have you done to your hand?
Spinks Grazed it.

Kingsley catches hold of Spinks's hand and examines it

Kingsley You've been fighting.
Spinks I wouldn't call it fighting. I threw a few, that's all. Get some ice, will you?

Kingsley exits into the kitchen

Spinks blows on his knuckles and straightens his tie

Kingsley returns with the ice tray. Spinks wraps the ice in his handkerchief and applies it to his hand

Kingsley I haven't heard anything about this. Where was it?
Spinks You won't laugh?
Kingsley No.
Spinks (*after a pause*) Church.

Kingsley laughs

You said you wouldn't laugh.
Kingsley Sorry. I couldn't help it. Fighting in church, Spinks. Shame on you.
Spinks Well, I wouldn't call it a church — just a room over the Co-op.
Kingsley What happened?
Spinks I finally blew, didn't I. First there was the kissing — they call it the kiss of peace but there was far too much of it for my liking ...
Kingsley You object to that, do you?
Spinks I do between men.
Kingsley Is that what started it?
Spinks No, there was a lot I didn't agree with but I kept my temper. There was the faith healing for a start; they really got worked up about that, throwing their crutches in the air, discarding their surgical appliances ... You'd have called it mass hysteria, except there was only seven of them. They had this faith healer with warts — always laying his hands on you. I couldn't help thinking, if he was such a great healer, why couldn't he get rid of those warts? But that didn't seem to have occurred to them. He was supposed to be curing Brother Robert's prostate but he still had to go out three times during the service ...
Kingsley So you decided to go in for a little laying on of hands on your own account, did you, Spinks?
Spinks It was Brother Jonathan's fault. He certainly changed his opinion of me. When I first arrived he said he saw me as a tongue of fire, and a cleansing stream. He never left me alone, breathing all over me and smelling strongly of peppermints. Always talking about Mother; never stopped talking about her — never let it rest.
Kingsley What about your mother?
Spinks He kept asking me if I wanted to see her again; apparently he knew someone who could arrange it — at a price.
Kingsley What did you say?
Spinks I said not at the moment — I still haven't got her that marble headstone. But he wouldn't leave it alone. Then after today's collection his mood changed dramatically. He ran his minces over the plate and he and Brother Robert started clucking and shaking their heads and looking at me. And saying, "God loves a cheerful giver", and "What profiteth a man if he should gain the whole world and lose his own soul?" Well, you know how I hate having the Bible quoted at me. I had enough of that from the old lady. I couldn't take any more — so I told them.

Kingsley (*staring*) Told them what?

Spinks I told them I hadn't got any money. That it was a rumour that had got out of hand.

Kingsley Spinks!

Spinks I was sick of the deception, Kingsley. I've never told so many lies in my life. I thought confession was good for the soul. But Brother Jonathan didn't see it in that light. He lost his temper. He called me a dissembler, a double dealer — and a transgressor. And said, "I spit upon your raiment and cast you forth." That was when I dropped Brother Jonathan.

Kingsley (*grinning*) Brother Jonathan, the elder?

Spinks Yeah, and then Brother Robert — and he's got an enlarged prostate. If they bring charges I could be in trouble. These fists could be considered lethal weapons.

Kingsley I don't see why. They weren't lethal in the ring. You only have to show them your record to prove you're harmless. But they won't bring any charges, Spinks. They'll elect to turn the other cheek. And do you know why? Because they couldn't afford the publicity. It was a scam. Church of the New Faithful — it was just a front. And was Dawn present at this confession?

Spinks Yeah.

Kingsley Well, it's the last we'll see of her.

Spinks Do you think so?

Kingsley Now she knows there isn't any money — certainly.

Spinks I don't know about that. She's never asked for any money — not once.

Kingsley No, she gets her sister to do it — or Brother Jonathan. If she comes back here now, Spinks — I'll stand bare-arsed in Woolworth's window.

Spinks She tore up the will.

Kingsley She didn't tear up the will — she crumpled it.

Spinks What's the difference?

Kingsley Crumpled is not the same as torn. Crumpled can be straightened. And you did straighten it. And she knew you would. What she doesn't know is that the document is worthless.

Spinks Not exactly.

Kingsley What do you mean, not exactly? Dead you're worth exactly what you are alive. Bugger all. The State will have to bury you to avoid you rotting by the dustbins.

Spinks That's not true, Kingsley. I'm worth a hundred thousand.

Kingsley What?

Spinks If I have an accident. You gave me the idea. I've insured my life. So all I have to do is step off that balcony — and she's worth a hundred grand.

Kingsley stares at him in amazed silence

Kingsley (*finally*) And are you contemplating that course of action, Spinks?

Spinks I might be. That poor girl trusted me. She gave me her love. And you know how I treated her. I owe her something.

Kingsley I knew it! You've finally flipped. All that pummelling in the ring has finally had its effect. You're going to kill yourself for a woman. (*He breaks off*) Wait a minute. How did you get that sort of cover—at your age? The period must be extremely short.

Spinks It is.

Kingsley So the jumping bit isn't too far off …

Spinks No.

Kingsley (*studying Spinks*) Premiums must be high.

Spinks They are.

Kingsley But how can you afford them? You're broke.

Spinks Not exactly.

Kingsley Don't keep saying "Not exactly" — it makes me nervous.

Spinks I do have some money.

Kingsley How much?

Spinks (*after a hesitation*) Five thousand pounds.

Kingsley sits down abruptly

Kingsley But you can't have. You're on Social Security. Your thumb's coming out of your glove. You have to give the clenched fist salute!

Spinks It's not mine. It's Mother's. I found it in a shoe box.

Kingsley Five thousand pounds! And you never let on. I thought we were friends. When I think of the times I've been cold and hungry. When I've had to beg you for the price of a loaf of bread. And all the time you had this money, and there wasn't even a hint — not a flicker, not even a glimmer from you.

Spinks Well, I wouldn't have had it long if I'd glimmered, would I? Besides, it's not mine — it's Mother's.

Kingsley She doesn't need it now.

Spinks She does. She left it for the marble headstone — and the carved cherubs fluttering over an open Bible, with a black marble surround and green chippings.

Kingsley What's wrong with a simple wooden cross?

Spinks She'd find a lot wrong with a simple wooden cross.

Kingsley And she'd find a lot wrong with you spending her money on a woman. (*He frowns*) How did you arrange all this?

Spinks My financial adviser did it.

Kingsley (*staring*) I'm your financial adviser.

Spinks I mean a proper one. She's been coming in the afternoon — during your siesta.

Kingsley She? I didn't know anything about this. You've never mentioned her.

Spinks Haven't I? She read about my good fortune in the paper — and offered her services.

Kingsley What's she like?

Spinks She's an independent consultant. Very business-like. Calls herself Ms.

Kingsley Ms?

Spinks Yeh. Ms. She's divorced. Her marriage never had a chance — sacrificed it for her career.

Kingsley Did she?

Spinks Working all hours. Never at home. Devoting all her time to her clients.

Kingsley And is she devoting all her time to you?

Spinks Some of it.

Kingsley She seems to have told you a lot about herself. Is she attractive?

Spinks You could say that. Nice legs. Smart. Dark suits — short skirts — padded shoulders.

Kingsley Dark suits — padded shoulders. You could be in trouble, Spinks. You know what you've got there, don't you? (*Darkly*) Power dressing.

Spinks Power dressing. What's that?

Kingsley It's part of the trend, Spinks. Part of the woman's movement to dominate and subdue men, and supplant them in the workplace.

Spinks Get away. Power dressing. Never heard it called that before. She gave me some very sound advice.

Kingsley How can she advise you? You haven't got any money.

Spinks She doesn't know that. I'm keeping her at arm's length at the moment.

Kingsley Then what's the point of it all?

Spinks I enjoy talking to her.

Kingsley My God! You're thinking about it, aren't you? Aren't two women enough? You've got more faces than a church clock, Spinks. I never had you down for promiscuous.

Spinks I fight against it, Kingsley. But I just can't help myself. I keep getting temptation thrown in my path.

Kingsley And you seem totally incapable of resisting it.

Spinks Well, you know what the old sheikh said. "God wouldn't have given us these desires, if he didn't want us to enjoy them."

Kingsley (*fiercely*) Don't quote "The Perfumed Garden" to me.

Spinks Well, that's what started it. That and the fact that everyone around here was at it but me. Him across the landing, assuring me he enjoyed a full sex life despite severe back problems that's kept him off work for years.

Then there's the couple upstairs banging away on the bleeding carpet ever since they had the bed repossessed. And even those pigeons out there have the gall to do it on my railings. The only one who wasn't getting his share, was me. Can you blame me for making up for lost time?

Kingsley But you didn't have to go to these lengths, Spinks. Not with your mother's money. You could have gone up West. Stopped at a five star hotel. Drunk champagne with a high-class tart. Made love in a four-poster bed — and still had change out of five hundred. Why did you have to complicate things?

Spinks Because I didn't want that, Kingsley. Well, I wanted that, but I wanted something else.

Kingsley Love? Don't tell me it's love again.

Spinks (*earnestly*) Kingsley, you're supposed to be an expert on women. If there hadn't been that piece in the paper — and no talk of any money. I mean, if I'd met Dawn in the supermarket by chance — and invited her back here. Do you think she'd have come?

Kingsley (*after a pause*) You know the answer to that as well as I do — or you wouldn't have asked the question. Now, I suggest we take what's left of your mother's money and have a bloody good time. (*Pause*) Where do you keep it?

Spinks (*guardedly*) Some at the bank — and some here.

Kingsley Here? Is it safe?

Spinks It is at the moment.

Kingsley Where do you keep it?

Spinks (*loftily*) That's for me to know — and you to find out.

Kingsley looks around slowly

Kingsley It's in the teapot, isn't it?

Spinks (*starting*) What? Why would I keep it in the teapot? It would get soggy.

Kingsley I notice you never use that teapot. But you always look in it when you come in. I've often wondered why.

Spinks No-one in his right mind would keep his money in a teapot.

Kingsley And there was something else. When the fire alarm went a few weeks ago, and I came up to fetch you. You appeared, almost bollock naked, clutching that same teapot. I should have known then. How much have you got in there?

Spinks About a thousand.

Kingsley A thousand! Then let's get out and spend it, you mean bugger.

Spinks No, it's for Dawn. To get some new clobber. Do you know that poor girl's darning her underwear?

Kingsley Spinks, you haven't been listening. She's not coming back.

There is the sound of the front door opening. Spinks and Kingsley look at each other and then at the hall door

    Dawn enters. She looks distressed. She stands in the threshold

Kingsley (*coldly*) How did you get in?
Dawn Arthur's given me a key.
Kingsley I thought I was the key holder.
Spinks Now there's two of you.
Kingsley It seems to be getting crowded around here.
Dawn Arthur, I want to speak to you.
Kingsley Well, speak. Spinks has no secrets from me.
Spinks Dawn, I'm sorry about what happened.
Dawn I was so ashamed.
Spinks How's Brother Jonathan?
Dawn In Casualty.
Spinks I didn't mean to hit him quite so hard. He went down like a roll of lino. I'm sorry, Dawn.
Dawn You don't need to apologize, Arthur. I'm glad he's in Casualty.
Spinks What!

Dawn's eyes are shining with tears

Dawn I was proud of you. I've never seen you like that before. And you were right. They'd turned our church into a den of thieves. You were like our Lord in the temple.
Spinks But what I said about the money — you didn't mind?
Dawn I only minded what they were trying to do to you. (*She kisses Spinks*)

Kingsley stares at Dawn in bewilderment

    (*Seeing Kingsley*) Gosh! I must look a mess. I'd better tidy my face …

    Dawn dabs her eyes and exits towards the bathroom

Spinks (*after a pause*) Well, that's a surprise …
Kingsley (*scowling*) I still don't believe it.
Spinks No, but then I don't think they'll believe it when they see you standing bare-arsed in Woolworth's window, Kingsley.

    Spinks guides Kingsley out into the hall

There is the sound of the front door slamming

Spinks returns and throws a victory punch

Dawn returns

Dawn Has he gone?

Spinks Yeah.

Dawn You see too much of him, Arthur. He'll drag you down to his level. He's the sort.

Spinks He's all right. I've got used to him.

Dawn You've outgrown him, Arthur. You've changed. You're so much better than he is.

Spinks (*uneasily*) I wouldn't be too sure about that, Dawn. And he's all right, once you get to know him.

Dawn Not according to my sister. She remembers him from Bromley. She said he had a very unsavoury reputation there.

Spinks Well, he has an unsavoury reputation here. But it's just the drink.

Dawn No, it wasn't the drink in Bromley, Arthur. It was something much worse.

Spinks What?

Dawn She wouldn't say, but it was a scandal.

Spinks Well, I wouldn't take too much notice of your sister — she is inclined to exaggerate.

Dawn Why? Have you met her, Arthur?

Spinks Met her? (*Cautiously*) Has she said I've met her?

Dawn She hasn't said anything. Have you, Arthur?

Spinks Well, I've spoken to her on the phone a few times …

Dawn But you haven't met her?

Spinks No, I've refused to see her.

Dawn That surprises me. Most men can't refuse Donna anything.

Spinks I'm not most men, Dawn. I told her not to come round. She's too mercenary for my liking. She's had your money, now she wants mine — if I had any, that is.

Dawn laughs and kisses him

Dawn You can stop that now, Arthur. Brother Jonathan isn't here.

Spinks What?

Dawn Oh, I don't blame you for saying what you did. It was the only way to get them off your back.

Spinks But you weren't taken in … ?

Dawn Arthur, it was in all the papers. They wouldn't print a story like that without checking the facts. It wouldn't be responsible journalism.

Spinks (*after a pause*) No, I suppose not. (*Pause*) So I didn't fool you for a moment?

Dawn Good heavens! No. Though I understood why you did it. Why you acted like that — even with me. It's because you're tired of people wanting you just for your money. It's a thing you can never be sure about, isn't it, Arthur?

Spinks takes a deep breath

Spinks It is the terrible dilemma that people in my position face. A dilemma all rich men face. Is it me, or the money?

Dawn It's you Arthur — I want you for yourself. (*She embraces him*) I've been reading that book, Arthur.

Spinks What book?

Dawn You know what book. The book that's not about gardening.

Spinks You shouldn't be reading that. It's not mine — it's Kingsley's.

Dawn (*whispering softly in Spinks's ear*) Do you know what it said? "An ideal man must be of good presence and excel in beauty all around him — be of good shape, and a slave to his promise." That's you, Arthur.

Spinks (*wincing*) I wouldn't say that, Dawn.

Dawn How do you see me, Arthur?

Spinks (*huskily*) I see the perfect waist — the large, dark eyes — the cheeks of perfect oval — the neck of a gazelle — the plump breasts standing out like hyacinths — lips fresh and red, like a gory sabre, and a forehead like the moon at night.

Dawn moves to the hall door

Dawn Should we go into the garden?

Spinks We're ten floors up … (*he stops*) Oh yeah.

Dawn smiles and exits

Spinks stares after Dawn. The phone rings. He answers it

Spinks Hallo? (*He lowers his voice*) No. Sorry, Donna. Not today. Something's cropped up.

Dawn (*off*) Arthur …

Spinks What? A woman's voice? Well, I know it's a woman's voice. It's my financial consultant — advising me on my portfolio. I've got to go. Bye. (*He replaces the phone and shakes his head*) No doubt about it — it gets easier … (*He moves to the door. He hesitates, then returns and picks up the teapot. He glances at his mother's picture, then places it face downwards*)

Spinks exits with the teapot

The Lights fade

The CURTAIN *falls*

Spinks's flat. A few days later. Evening

The room has never been tidier. The answerphone light is flashing

When the CURTAIN *rises, Spinks is slipping on a tie*

Kingsley enters from the kitchen, spearing beans from a tin

Spinks (*frowning*) Do you have to do that?

Kingsley I was hungry.

Spinks That's no excuse. You don't have to eat beans from a tin, even if you're starving. (*He re-arranges the cushions*)

Kingsley You used to do it.

Spinks Did I? Well, my standards are a little higher these days. I was letting myself go — probably the company I was keeping.

Kingsley Do you mean me?

Spinks Do you know one of the saddest things in a friendship, Kingsley? It's when you find that you've outgrown that friend — when you have nothing left to talk about.

Kingsley I've got plenty to talk about.

Spinks That's interesting.

Kingsley I'm interesting.

Spinks Well, go and be interesting somewhere else. When you've finished those beans — hop it. I've got my financial adviser coming.

Kingsley Ah, that explains all this activity. (*Pause*) She's working late, isn't she?

Spinks I'm a valued client.

Kingsley Valued! If only she knew.

Spinks Well, she doesn't, so hop it.

Kingsley How do you get away with it, Spinks?

Spinks (*grinning*) I've convinced her I'm a nervous investor — and she wants me to speculate. The debate could go on for some time. There's some Twiglets in a bowl in the kitchen, and some wine cooling in the fridge — bring them through, would you? (*He arranges the room to his satisfaction during the following*)

Kingsley exits into the kitchen and returns with the bowl and the wine

Kingsley I still don't know what you find to talk about.

Spinks Well, at the moment she wants to know if I prefer capital growth to revenue yield. In other words, do I want it now or later?

Kingsley (*considering*) I'd say now, every time. You never know what's
  going to happen.

Spinks And that shows your working class origins, Kingsley.

Kingsley How do you make that out?

Spinks You'll find that the middle classes — i.e. those with the money —
  defer present pleasure for future gains. Whereas, the working classes prefer
  instant gratification. That's what Tessa says.

Kingsley Oh, it's Tessa now, is it? And what are you opting for this evening?
  Are you going to defer your pleasure, Spinks — or go for instant
  gratification?

Spinks That remains to be seen, Kingsley.

Kingsley You've become a smooth bastard, Spinks.

Spinks Do you know what I think you resent most, Kingsley? It's my easy
  way with women.

Kingsley Easy way! They think you've got money!

Spinks I don't think it's that, not now.

Kingsley You don't?

Spinks No.

Kingsley You don't think Donna Miller's after your money?

Spinks Well, at first, yes. But now she's got to know me she finds herself
  drawn to my personality. She said so.

Kingsley Personality! I had a budgerigar with more personality than you've
  got.

Spinks And there's something else … (*He looks in the mirror*) Donna says
  I've grown into my looks.

Kingsley (*staring*) You've done what?

Spinks Grown into my looks.

Kingsley What does that mean?

Spinks There's a time in everyone's life when they grow into their looks —
  when everything comes together — and they finally look their best. (*He
  glances at Kingsley*) I think it happened to you some time ago, Kingsley.
  (*He returns to the mirror*) Whereas, I appear to have achieved mine
  recently. What do you think?

Kingsley (*studying Spinks*) All I can say is this, if you're looking your best
  now what the hell did you look like before?

Spinks God! You're so jealous. It shows in every pore.

Kingsley And what happens when Donna finds out you haven't won the
  lottery? You think your looks are going to save you then? Don't forget the
  date on the cheque grows ever nearer.

Spinks It may not make any difference. (*He parts his hair carefully*)

Kingsley There you go again, Spinks! You're going around here with your
  thumb up your bum and your brain in neutral. Why do you think it may not
  make any difference?

Spinks Well, as I said, I know it was the money at first, but women — even
gold diggers — have a history of standing by their men in adversity. It can
bring the best out of them.

Kingsley (*patiently*) That may be true, Spinks. But women who stand by
their men in the bad times, have also enjoyed the good times. The same
cannot be said for Donna Miller. What good times has she had around here?

Spinks You'd be surprised. She's had a lot of good times.

Kingsley (*staring*) Let me get this straight. You think she actually enjoys it?

Spinks (*indignantly*) Of course she enjoys it.

Kingsley I don't believe it. I bet you creak more than the bed, Spinks.

Spinks Look, do you mind, Kingsley. Tessa will be here soon.

Kingsley And suppose one of the others rolls up while she's here?

Spinks They won't. I've sent Dawn up west to get herself some new clobber
— and Donna's having drinks with her creditors.

Kingsley You seem to have got everything organized, Spinks.

Spinks I'm keeping a few plates in the air at the moment, Kingsley.

Kingsley rises to leave. He glances across at the sideboard

Kingsley By the way, your light's flashing — you've got a call.

Spinks Probably Tessa on her mobile. She usually rings first. (*He presses
a button on the answerphone*)

Voice (*voiceover from phone*) You have one call.

Dawn (*voiceover from phone*) Hallo, Arthur. It's Dawn. I got through earlier
than I expected — so I got off at your station. I'll be round in a few minutes.
Love you …

Silence

Spinks Gawd! I can't be doing with her now. I've got Tessa coming round.

Kingsley (*grinning*) You should be able to handle it, Spinks. After all,
you've got an easy way with women. (*He makes for the door*)

Spinks Hang about, Kingsley. (*He takes some money from the teapot*) Look,
wait for Dawn downstairs. When she comes, say I'm out. Take her to the
Chinese — I'll be along later. Here's some money.

Kingsley (*nervously*) I can't do that.

Spinks Why not?

Kingsley I don't like her.

Spinks I'm not asking you to marry her — just take her to the Chinese.

Kingsley I can't.

Spinks Why not?

Kingsley I've got things to do.

Spinks You never have anything to do.

Kingsley I have tonight. I've got a lot on.
Spinks You haven't got anything on.
Kingsley What would we talk about? We have nothing in common …

Kingsley moves around the room, looking strangely uncomfortable. Spinks regards him curiously

Spinks My God. Just look at you. You're all over the place like a mad woman's sheet. All the advice you've been giving me and I've suddenly realized something. You're afraid of them.
Kingsley Who's them?
Spinks Women.
Kingsley (*evasively*) No, I'm not. I just think there's something odd about her, Spinks.
Spinks You mean, one black note short of a keyboard?
Kingsley No. Something else. Something I can't put my finger on. I felt it right from the start. Something sinister.
Spinks You haven't forgiven her for coming back, have you? And you still haven't stood bare-arsed in Woolworth's window.
Kingsley I haven't stood bare-arsed in Woolworth's window because she came back for the wrong reasons — she still thinks you've got money.
Spinks I won't hear a word against her, Kingsley. She believes in me — the least I can do is believe in her. And I'll tell you something else: she could say a lot about you — only she's too much of a lady.
Kingsley What do you mean?
Spinks She knows why you left Bromley. And it was something unsavoury …

Kingsley is about to speak when the door opens slowly

Donna stands before them — at least it is Dawn, in the image of Donna. She is heavily made up and dressed more provocatively than ever. She is wearing a tight, short skirt and plunging neckline. She has bright red lips and painted nails

Dawn Did I startle you?
Spinks Yes, you did as a matter of fact …
Kingsley Good-night, Spinks.
Spinks Kingsley.
Kingsley It looks to me as though the plates are beginning to fall, Spinks.

Kingsley exits

Dawn What did he mean by that?

Spinks No idea. I wasn't expecting you.

Dawn I finished early. (*Pause*) How do I look?

Spinks Beautiful as ever. (*He kisses her*) But you shouldn't be here. Dawn's on her way.

Dawn What?

Spinks What's she going to think? You dressed like that. I've always said I've never laid a glove on you. She'll be madly jealous. Kingsley thinks she's one black note short of a keyboard, as it is.

Dawn (*after a pause*) What do you think?

Spinks Well, she may be your sister, but you must admit she can be a little strange. You know how agitated she gets. And she'll certainly get agitated if she finds you here.

Dawn turns away

What's the matter?

Dawn (*in a tense voice*) Agitated! I was born agitated. Agitated is my middle name. (*She turns to face him*)

Spinks Why are you talking like that? (*He stops*) My God! It's you.

Dawn (*bitterly*) Yes. Dawn — that's one note short of a keyboard. The Dawn who's a little strange. The Dawn you said you loved.

Spinks Why did you have to dress like that?

Dawn (*tearfully*) I thought you'd like me like this. I thought that's why you wanted me to buy new clothes — because you found me dull. I thought if I was more like Donna ... That's what you like, isn't it, Arthur? You lied to me. (*She moves away from him*)

Spinks (*reaching for her arm*) Dawn — listen ——

Dawn makes a break for the balcony

(*Catching hold of her*) I didn't mean what I said, Dawn. You know what she's like. I was just being diplomatic.

Dawn (*struggling*) You'd say anything but your prayers, Arthur. I can't trust you any more ...

Dawn breaks free and dashes from the room. Spinks follows

We hear a door bang

Spinks (*off*) Come out of there, for God's sake! Let's talk about this ...

The phone starts to ring

Spinks returns, mopping his brow. He answers the phone

(*Into the phone*) Hallo? ... Donna! Where are you? ... Well, come up for God's sake. ... I know she's here, but it doesn't matter now. She knows — and she's suicidal. ... I told her. I thought she was you and I gave the game away. Come up and talk to her, for God's sake. Reason with her. She's bolted the door on me. And it's a long drop from that window. ... What? Don't worry. I'll stay away from her ...

Kingsley enters

Spinks puts the phone down and closes the door behind Kingsley

Kingsley What's all the shouting about, Spinks?

Spinks takes a deep drink from the vodka bottle

What's the matter?
Spinks That wasn't Donna. That was Dawn. I told her everything. She went berserk. She's locked herself in the bedroom. I've destroyed her, Kingsley. She says she's going to jump.

Kingsley turns to the door

No. Donna says we must stay away from her.

Spinks takes another drink. Kingsley watches him

Kingsley I thought you were the one who was going to jump?
Spinks (*wildly*) Perhaps I should.
Kingsley What?
Spinks After what I've done, that's what I deserve — and she'd be provided for. (*He opens the glass door*) I've done a terrible thing, Kingsley — a terrible thing. I can't face the world if she dies — I'd sooner jump ... (*He moves on to the balcony*)
Kingsley (*calmly*) Don't be a prick, Spinks. Come away from there — with your eyesight, you could fall.

Spinks returns angrily

Spinks There's nothing wrong with my eyesight.
Kingsley Come and sit down, Spinks. It won't hurt to wait. We don't want her landing on top of you, do we? And as for facing the world — it isn't pleasant but it usually gets faced, and it's better than being dead.

Spinks sits and buries his head in his hands

(*Moving the vodka bottle*) I'm going to make you some coffee.

Kingsley exits into kitchen

Spinks' shoulders begin to shake

Donna enters. She is wearing a raincoat and carrying a shoulder bag. She looks serious. She closes the door quietly behind her

Donna Where is she now?

Spinks She's still in the bedroom. (*He moves to the hall door*)

Donna No, leave her. Don't go near her. I've seen her like this before. She won't want to see you.

Spinks I can understand that. Do you think she'll do it?

Donna I don't know. She tried it once before. And she's worse now. All that worry over the house — now this. I told you, we should have sent her away, on a cruise or something — but you wouldn't.

Spinks Suppose I could put it right? The house — so that she could keep it. And the cruise. Give her the money.

Donna Money doesn't mean anything to her.

Spinks But the house does. And she's always wanted to travel. I could make a cheque out now. You could slip it under the door.

Donna (*after a hesitation*) She may be insulted.

Spinks It would show I was concerned. I could write, "I love you", on the back of the cheque ... (*He busies himself with the cheque book*) Suppose I write a cheque for a hundred thousand, and write "I love you" on the back of the cheque?

Donna (*staring*) A hundred thousand! Could you cover it? I thought all your money was tied up?

Spinks (*glancing at the balcony*) I could cover a hundred thousand ... (*He hands the completed cheque to Donna*)

Donna I can't guarantee this will work. She's very stubborn.

Kingsley enters with a cup of coffee

Donna turns and sees Kingsley. She starts in surprise. They stare at each other

Donna What are you doing here? I thought you'd left.

Kingsley Is that another cheque, Spinks?

Spinks She's taking it to Dawn, Kingsley. It's our only hope.

Donna makes for the door. Kingsley moves to stand in her way

Kingsley Where are you going?

Spinks To the bedroom — she's going to reason with her.

Kingsley But she's not there, Spinks.

Spinks What? How do you know? Did you hear her go? I didn't hear her go. How do you know she's not there?

Kingsley Because she's here.

Spinks What?

Kingsley You've never seen them together have you, Spinks?

Spinks Well, no ——

Kingsley And you never will. Because there's only one of them. And I say thank God for that! One's enough.

Spinks No, you're wrong, Kingsley. Dawn's bolted herself in …

Spinks exits into the hall

Donna and Kingsley regard each other in silence

Spinks returns, looking puzzled

Spinks You're right. She's not there. How did you know?

Kingsley (*sighing*) Do you need the building to fall on you, Spinks? You want proof? She said she thought I'd left — but it was Dawn who saw me leave. And to my knowledge you only have one spare key — and you gave that to Dawn.

Spinks Right.

Kingsley Then how did she get in?

Spinks (*after a hesitation*) Dawn must have left the door open.

Donna The door was open.

Spinks There you are! Donna didn't need a key.

Kingsley She didn't need a key because she was here the whole time.

Spinks You're talking in riddles. Kingsley. The drink's finally softened your brain. She didn't need a key because the door was open!

Kingsley (*after a pause*) So there wouldn't be a key in her bag?

Spinks Of course not. Dawn has the key.

Kingsley Should we see? (*He snatches the bag from Donna*)

Donna fights to get the bag back. Spinks grabs the bag from Kingsley

Spinks You're out of order, Kingsley. You don't look in a lady's handbag.

Kingsley She's no lady.

Spinks (*breathing heavily*) That's it, Kingsley — you've gone too far.

Kingsley What are you going to do — drop me?
Spinks (*after a hesitation*) No. I'm going to put your mind at rest. I'm going to make you ashamed of yourself. We'll look in the bag. I know Donna won't mind ... (*He rummages through the bag*)

Donna turns away. Unseen, she makes a call on her mobile phone

Because, you see, you don't know everything. You don't know about the phone calls. I was talking to both of them, Kingsley ... (*He produces the key from the handbag and his voice dies away*)

The phone rings. Spinks snatches up the receiver

(*Into the phone*) Hallo? Dawn?

Donna turns. She is talking into her mobile

Donna Hallo, Arthur.
Spinks (*triumphantly*) It's Dawn! What did I tell you! Look, I'm sorry, Dawn.
Donna (*as Dawn*) So am I, Arthur. I'm afraid you were mistaken in me — but what I find even more heartbreaking — I was mistaken in you ...
Spinks I can explain. Where are you?
Donna Right here, Spinks. (*She taps Spinks on the shoulder*)

Spinks turns and sees Dawn talking into the mobile. His jaw drops

(*Shrugging*) Modern technology, Spinks — it'll be the death of us.
Kingsley Now do you get it?
Spinks Yeah, I get it. (*In an awed tone*) She's got a split personality. She needs treatment.
Kingsley Christ, no! She hasn't got a split personality. I don't know her reasons but that's not one of them.
Donna (*smiling*) Don't you? No, I haven't got a split personality, Spinks. But when I saw your picture in the paper, I knew it wasn't going to be easy. I saw that mean, furtive face with the shortsighted stare and I knew it was going to be like getting blood out of a stone. I knew I'd have to come again, and again, and again ...
Spinks (*bitterly*) So it was the money. And I thought it was my dashing good looks and exciting lifestyle.
Donna Exciting? (*She crosses and looks into Spinks's face*) I've seen more life on a fishmonger's slab, Spinks.
Spinks (*shocked*) What?

Kingsley As Mr Spinks's financial adviser I shall insist, of course, on cancelling the cheques, which were obtained under false pretences …

Spinks (*harshly*) Why bother? Why keep up the pretence, Kingsley? Tell her the truth. The joke's on you, darling. There isn't any money — there never was. You did all this for nothing. I made the whole thing up. You shouldn't believe all you read in the papers.

Donna regards Spinks in silence for a moment

Donna Don't insult my intelligence, Spinks. Do you think I went into this without making enquiries? I spoke to people around here — some had actually seen the cheque.

Spinks What? (*He stares helplessly at Kingsley*)

Donna They were able to tell me the exact amount. They also said you were as tight as a duck's arse in a thunderstorm. It's typical you'd deny it. (*She shakes her head*) It should have been easy — like robbing a blind man. (*She glances at Kingsley*) But I didn't allow for the seeing dog. (*She moves to the door*)

Spinks There's some money in the teapot.

Donna (*after a hesitation*) How much?

Spinks A few hundred. Take it. You've earned it.

Kingsley Spinks!

Donna If you think I came for a few hundred … (*She stops. Shrugging*) Well, why not …? (*She takes the money*)

Kingsley (*quietly*) Who's unsavoury now?

Donna (*turning*) Oh, I didn't tell you about our friend, did I, Spinks? He was a pillar of the community in Bromley, attended church with his wife and family, sang in the choir — very active in youth work. That was until he became too active with one of the youths. Then he had to leave. His wife couldn't live with it and she kicked him out. He couldn't live with it and started to drink. He's gay, Spinks — and he doesn't like it. He may hate me, but he hates himself more. Isn't that right, Kingsley?

Kingsley remains silent. Donna smiles and moves to the door

(*Holding up the money*) Thanks, Spinks.

Spinks And you never fancied me at all?

Donna Spinks, I wouldn't fancy you if you were studded in diamonds and peed champagne.

Donna exits

There is the sound of the front door slamming. Spinks and Kingsley sit in silence for a moment

Spinks Did you hear that? More life on a fishmonger's slab. Doesn't do much for your self-esteem, does it. (*He stops and stares abruptly at Kingsley*) Gay?

Kingsley (*grimly*) I'm not discussing it, Spinks.

Spinks Gay. I must say I'm surprised. I've always found you bloody depressing.

Kingsley I said I'm not discussing it.

Spinks You're right. What's the use of discussing it? Life's too short. It's like that lift out there, Kingsley. It's a short trip and we all get out at different floors — so what's the point in starting a conversation. God! Did you hear what she said? She wouldn't fancy me if I was studded in diamonds and peed champagne. That was very wounding. The old lady was right. You can't trust them.

Kingsley "Expect nothing from life and you won't be disappointed." Isn't that what she said?

Spinks She drummed it into me, Kingsley. (*He gives a rueful smile*) That's why I could never beat Fletcher. I was as good as he was. I could punch as hard. But I never felt good enough. Know what I mean? I never felt — worthy. She did that to me.

Kingsley Let's have a drink.

Spinks You drink too much.

Kingsley pours. He becomes aware that Spinks is watching him

Kingsley What are you staring at?

Spinks You don't fancy me, do you?

Kingsley No.

Spinks That's a relief. Mind you, I don't know why I asked. Who does? (*He drinks*) Did you hear what she said?

Kingsley Yes. She'd seen more life on a fishmonger's slab.

Spinks (*frowning*) No, I mean, that she'd spoken to people who'd actually seen the cheque.

Kingsley Well, that's more than we have.

Spinks We don't seem to be able to deny it. We've certainly started something.

Kingsley We? Don't involve me. You started it. And you should be pleased she didn't believe you. You saw how vindictive she can be. She'd tell everyone and we'd get lynched.

Spinks Don't worry. I'm finished with it after tonight.

Kingsley Good.

Spinks Once she's been …

Kingsley You're not still going through with that — not now!

Spinks (*grinning*) All that power-dressing? Of course I'm going through with it.

Kingsley replenishes their glasses

Kingsley You're a rogue, Spinks.
Spinks I know. And don't think I don't feel guilty about it.
Kingsley It doesn't stop you doing it, though, does it?
Spinks Has feeling guilty ever stopped anyone doing it, Kingsley?
Kingsley (*smiling*) You're learning, Spinks — you're learning. (*He looks sadly into his glass*) But they'll find out — they always do. There'll be a reckoning — there always is. I know that from Bromley. Then what are we going to do?

Spinks considers

Spinks (*grinning*) Perhaps that'll be the time to surface in Tangier, Kingsley … (*He raises his glass*)

Kingsley grins. They touch glasses

Spinks ⎫
Kingsley ⎬ (*together*) Tangier …

The Curtain *falls*

FURNITURE AND PROPERTY LIST

ACT I

SCENE 1

On stage:	Electric fire
	Old dining-table
	Chairs
	Battered settee
	Coffee table
	Bin
	Sideboard. *On it*: bric-a-brac, old photographs, boxing trophies, teapot.
	In it: glasses, small fire extinguisher
	On all surfaces: pots, plates, clothes
	Telephone with answering machine. *Covering it*: shirt
	On wall: boxing gloves, mirror
	On all surfaces: pots, plates, clothes
	Newspaper, magnifying glass, open tin of beans and fork for **Spinks**

Off stage:	Newspaper (**Dawn**)
	Lottery ticket (**Kingsley**)

Personal:	**Kingsley**: bottle of Scotch, two cigars
	Spinks: five pound note, cologne bottle

SCENE 2

Re-set:	Tidy room

Set:	Nibbles
	Table set for dinner
	On sideboard: bottle of red wine
	Glass for **Kingsley**

Off stage:	Two plates of avocado
	Tea towel

Personal:	**Kingsley**: paperback book
	Spinks: handkerchief (carried throughout)

SCENE 3

Set: Brochures and bottle of vodka for **Kingsley**

ACT II

SCENE 1

Set: Goods on approval and "freebies"
                   Legal document and pen for **Spinks**

Off stage: Full pint of beer (**Kingsley**)
                   Shopping (**Dawn**)

Personal: **Kingsley**: small bottle of vodka

SCENE 2

Set: Glass for **Kingsley**

Off stage: Ice tray (**Kingsley**)

SCENE 3

Re-set: Tidy room

Off stage: Tin of beans, fork (**Kingsley**)
                   Bowl of Twiglets, bottle of wine (**Kingsley**)
                   Cup of coffee (**Kingsley**)

Personal: **Donna**: shoulder bag. In it: mobile phone, key
                   Spinks: cheque book

LIGHTING PLOT

Practical fittings required: electric fire, telephone answering machine light
One interior with exterior balcony backing. The same throughout

ACT I, SCENE 1

To open: General interior lighting with exterior balcony backing lit; autumn late
afternoon effect. Electric fire on

Cue 1   **Kingsley** pours whisky back into **Spinks**'s glass   (Page 15)
               Fade lights to black-out

ACT I, SCENE 2

To open: General interior lighting with exterior balcony backing lit: autumn evening
effect. Electric fire on

Cue 2   **Spinks**: "The woman who doesn't exist"   (Page 26)
               Fade lights to black-out

ACT I, SCENE 3

To open: General interior lighting with exterior balcony backing lit: autumn early
afternoon effect. Electric fire on

Cue 3   **Donna** begins to remove her ear-rings   (Page 36)
               Fade lights to black-out

ACT II, SCENE 1

To open: General interior lighting with exterior balcony backing lit: autumn
afternoon effect. Electric fire on

Cue 4   Heavy crash, off   (Page 46)
               Fade lights to black-out

ACT II, SCENE 2

To open: General interior lighting with exterior balcony backing lit: autumn afternoon setting. Electric fire on

Cue 5   **Spinks** exits with the teapot   (Page 54)
            Fade lights to black-out

ACT II, SCENE 3

To open: General interior lighting with exterior balcony backing dimly lit; autumn evening setting. Electric fire on, telephone answering machine light flashing

No cues

EFFECTS PLOT

ACT I

Cue 1	When ready *Sound of front door opening*	(Page 1)
Cue 2	**Kingsley**: "I'm taking you out tonight." *Phone rings*	(Page 5)
Cue 3	**Spinks**: "Well, that's not my problem." *Doorbell rings*	(Page 7)
Cue 4	**Spinks** peers out of the window *Front door slams*	(Page 12)
Cue 5	**Kingsley**: "We're sailing close to the wind here, Spinks." *Phone rings*	(Page 14)
Cue 6	**Kingsley**: "Then you move on, Spinks." *Doorbell*	(Page 18)
Cue 7	**Dawn** and **Spinks** drink *Loud banging from kitchen*	(Page 20)
Cue 8	**Dawn**: "No. Something's burning!" *Smoke drifts in from kitchen*	(Page 23)
Cue 9	**Kingsley** enters *Smoke effect from **Kingsley**'s coat*	(Page 23)
Cue 10	**Kingsley** enters *Smoke effect from tea towel*	(Page 23)
Cue 11	**Spinks**: "Someone to ring you late at night ——" *Phone rings*	(Page 26)
Cue 12	Voices of **Kingsley** and **Donna** are heard off *Front door slams*	(Page 31)

ACT II

Cue 13	**Kingsley** exits *Front door slams*	(Page 41)
Cue 14	**Spinks** leaves the will on a chair *Sound of front door opening*	(Page 41)
Cue 15	**Spinks** exits with **Dawn** *Heavy crash*	(Page 46)
Cue 16	**Kingsley**: "She's not coming back." *Sound of front door opening*	(Page 51)
Cue 17	**Spinks** guides **Kingsley** out into the hall *Front door slams*	(Page 52)
Cue 18	**Spinks** stares after **Dawn** *Phone rings*	(Page 72)
Cue 19	**Spinks** presses a button on the answerphone **Answerphone Voice** *and* **Dawn***'s voice as dialogue p. 57*	(Page 57)
Cue 20	**Spinks** follows **Dawn** out of the room *Door bangs*	(Page 59)
Cue 21	**Spinks** (*off*) "Let's talk about this ... " *Telephone rings*	(Page 59)
Cue 22	**Spinks** produces the key from the handbag *Telephone rings*	(Page 63)
Cue 23	**Donna** exits *Front door slams*	(Page 64)